CrazyAboutCacti andSucculents

Ray Rogers

EDITOR

Janet Marinelli
SERIES EDITOR

Sigrun Wolff Saphire
SENIOR EDITOR

Mark Tebbitt
SCIENCE EDITOR

Elizabeth Ennis
ART DIRECTOR

Joni Blackburn
COPY EDITOR

Steven Clemants
VICE-PRESIDENT,
SCIENCE &
PUBLICATIONS

Scot Medbury
PRESIDENT

Elizabeth Scholtz
DIRECTOR
EMERITUS

Handbook #184

Copyright © 2006 by Brooklyn Botanic Garden, Inc.

All-Region Guides, formerly *21st-Century Gardening Series,* are published three times a year at 1000 Washington Ave., Brooklyn, NY 11225.

Subscription included in Brooklyn Botanic Garden subscriber membership dues ($35 per year; $45 outside the United States).

ISBN 13: 978-1-889538-72-3
ISBN 10: 1-889538-72-8

Printed by Science Press, a division of Cadmus Communications. Printed on recycled paper.

Above: *Mammillaria prolifera.*
Cover: *Echeveria* 'Ebony'.

Crazy About Cacti and Succulents

Crazy About Cacti and Other Succulents

Ray Rogers

Cacti and other succulents used to leave me cold. Sure, I grew a few in my earlier years, including a nasty bunny ears (*Opuntia*) that projected its tiny, itchy, impossible-to-get-out little spines into me every time I got too close to it, and a dime-store cactus that went with me to college and met its demise during a high-spirited abduction prank. A few years later I was employed in public horticulture, but I still had little interaction with succulents, save for the specimens put before me as a "passer" (one of the quality-control agents, essentially) at the Philadelphia Flower Show. Some of my colleagues from those days may recall my standoff with a prominent member of the Philadelphia gardening community over the deficient (in my estimation) crown of thorns (*Euphorbia milii*) she wanted to enter in the show. Ouch.

So who would have thought that at the 2005 Philadelphia Flower Show I would become the ecstatic winner of the top prize for cacti and other succulents? What took me from stone cold to blazing hot? Every succulentophile has a reason for developing a passion for these spiny, fleshy, often bizarre- or even dead-looking members of the plant kingdom. For me the sparks that lit the fire were succulents presented at flower shows that came after the one that witnessed the crown of thorns incident. Succulent enthusiasts, some of them demigods of the Philadelphia Flower Show (and who were later to become good friends of mine), offered up expertly grown and beau-

Fleshy or spiny and often bizarre looking, succulents such as the show-worthy specimens at right often require a closer look to discover their intricate designs.

Though it looks much like a cactus, *Euphorbia horrida* 'Snowflake' is simply a succulent, a plant that has evolved to store water for times of drought.

tifully presented plants that, to my eye, took on new identities. I imagined "plates of squid" (*Euphorbia cylindrifolia* subspecies *tuberifera*) and "thorny cookie-press dough" (*Astrophytum ornatum*) and a host of other forms in these evocative, sculptural, fascinating plants. Soon after, I tried my hand at growing some, killing many but still willing to try to approximate the competitive successes I had admired.

A few of those earliest attempts are still with me, and some have become my consistently big winners at competitions. Many other specimens have joined the collection, more than a few of them acquired through the Philadelphia Cactus and Succulent Society, at sales or swaps or as kind gifts from my fellow members. For the past few years I have given programs on these objects of my passion and desire, and now here I am, the editor (and contributor, too; see "Grooming Cacti and Other Succulents for Exhibition," page 98) of a book on the subject.

I'm not alone in my love for these inhabitants of stupefyingly harsh, or, at the very least, seasonally unfavorable climates. In these pages you will find offerings by people who have explored their medicinal uses; who have elevated them into works of art though applying the methods and mind-set of bonsai; who take pleasure in growing them outdoors in cold climates or on roofs; and who have focused their efforts and enthusiasm on one facet of the jewel that is the world of cacti and other succulents.

Cacti and Other Succulents—the Basics

The broad term *succulent* describes plants from many plant families that store water against times of drought in specialized tissues, whether in fleshy leaves (such as those on a jade plant), stems (as with most cacti), or a stem-root structure known as a caudex (as with *Fockea crispa*, page 10). All cacti are succulents, as are the desert dwellers agaves, aloes, and many euphorbias, to name a few plants popular with gardeners.

Cacti, or more correctly, the family Cactaceae, are a subgroup of the succulent world. They are distinguished by flowers composed of many petals and stamens and by the presence of areoles, essentially lateral shoots that look like little round or oval cushions. Areoles give rise to spines, new shoots, flowers, and fruit.

One of the most striking features of a solitary (or nonbranching) cactus or succulent is its geometrical shape, which is due to the single growing point at the tip of the plant from which new stem and spines appear. Sometimes a genetic mutation gives rise to a crested or a monstrose cactus. A crested cactus has many growing points at its tip, forming fanlike patterns when the growing points occur in a straight line or convoluted patterns if the line is wavy (see ×*Graptoveria* 'Silver Star', page 71). In a monstrose cactus the mutation occurs on the entire plant, not merely at its tip. Growth points originate all over the stem or branches, causing very irregular growth. The resulting plant may bear little to no resemblance to other plants of the same species.

As a member of the cactus family, *Sulcorebutia heliosa* has areoles, specialized structures that give rise to spines, flowers, and fruit, as well as new shoots.

A Gardener's Guide to Cacti and Succulent Conservation

Janet Marinelli

Because cacti and other succulents, the camels of the plant kingdom, have special adaptations to store water, they often have swollen and bizarre-looking growth forms. To conserve precious moisture, leaf succulents, such as aloes, retain water in their fleshy foliage. Cacti often have no obvious leaves at all and store water in their engorged stems. Caudiciforms, called fat-bottom plants, have swollen stem bases at or below ground level. Add to this their often unique and spectacular flowers, and it's easy to understand why cacti and other succulents have captivated gardeners and collectors the world over for centuries. Today, dozens of succulent and cactus societies around the globe form one of the largest horticultural networks, and the plants are no longer the mania of a few obscure collectors.

Of the estimated 10,000 plant species in 30 families that are considered succulents, some 2,000 are threatened with global extinction in the wild, and many more are threatened regionally or nationally. Today, the greatest threat to succulents is shrinking habitat, particularly where development, agriculture, and mining have taken a heavy toll. However, as is the case for orchids and other horticulturally desirable plants, cacti and other succulents form the basis for a multimillion-dollar international industry. They are sold both as general houseplants and as botanical speci-

Though not endangered yet, a cactus like *Echinocereus fendleri*, hedgehog cactus, can quickly become threatened in the wild by illegal collection when it turns into a sought-after garden plant.

men plants for specialist collectors. Collection of plants from the wild for sale in the trade has been one of the main threats to certain species, and despite the development of sophisticated propagation techniques, this threat remains a major problem.

Wild-collected plants don't end up just in the greenhouses of obsessive hobbyists. Traffic North America, which monitors trade in imperiled plants and animals, estimates that between 1998 and 2001, nearly 100,000 succulents were dug up from the wild in Texas and Mexico to supply the landscaping market in Phoenix and Tucson alone. Ironically, the shift to xeriscaping, which uses a fraction of the water required by lawns, has led to a surge in demand for cacti and succulents—and indiscriminate removal of plants from the wild. What's more, some cacti and succulents face the limitations of their own biology, such as an extremely restricted range or habitat requirement, slow growth, or poor seed set.

By learning which cactus and succulent species are threatened with extinction in the wild and exercising care when purchasing plants, gardeners can play an important role in reducing the illegal sale of cacti and other succulents. Following are some suggestions.

Caudiciforms such as *Fockea crispa* are in great demand right now. Purchasing only nursery-propagated plants can prevent such species from becoming victims of unscrupulous international trade.

Growing rare succulents from seed is the best way to ensure that your plants have not been illegally collected from the wild.

- Don't buy *any* cacti or other succulent unless you are sure that it is nursery-grown and not collected from the wild. Ask suppliers about the plant's origin. When in doubt, don't buy. If gardeners reject wild-collected plants, the market for them will dry up and sellers will no longer offer them.
- Become aware of which cacti and other succulents are threatened with extinction, and be especially cautious when buying these. See the World Conservation Union's (IUCN) *Status Survey and Conservation Action Plan for Cactus and Succulent Plants* for detailed information on species of conservation concern (you can download the entire report at www.dererum.net/cssg/whoweare/actionplan.html).
- Be especially cognizant of which cacti and succulents are threatened by collection in the wild for international trade. Many of these plants are afforded protection by the Convention on International Trade in Endangered Species of Wild Fauna and Flora (CITES). Species listed in Appendix I of CITES, including scores of cacti, succulent euphorbias, and aloes, are considered to be at serious risk from *any* commercial trade, and thus *all* international trade in wild specimens is prohibited. Permits are necessary for legal international trade of any species listed in Appendix II, such as all cacti, succulent euphorbias, and pachypodiums that are not already listed in Appendix I. You can find the entire list of CITES-protected plants on the Internet at www.cites.org/eng/app/appendices.shtml. When purchasing a CITES-listed plant, ask to see import permits that demonstrate that the plant was imported

legally. If there is any question about the plant's legality, do not buy it.

- Be aware, too, that many succulents currently in great demand by collectors and quite fashionable in the horticulture trade, such as ceropegias (see page 44) and stapeliads (see page 52), are not now protected by CITES. The same is true for most caudiciforms, including adeniums, many of which are slow-growing in cultivation and therefore regularly collected from the wild for sale in the trade. Be sure to purchase only nursery-propagated specimens to prevent these species from becoming victims of international commerce.

- When growing a rare cactus or other succulent species, keep accurate records of when and from whom you get your plant or seeds, and ask your supplier for any pertinent data, such as collectors' numbers, the location where the plant or seed

Ceropegias such as *Ceropegia aristolochioides* have become extremely fashionable. To protect wild plants, purchase only nursery-propagated specimens.

Support the International Organization for Succulent Plant Study and other conservation-oriented groups to safeguard the future of spectacular plants such as the stapeliad *Tridentea virescens*.

was originally collected, etc. For some critically endangered species, private collections may become an important stockpile of germplasm for future conservation efforts, and such records increase the conservation value of your plants.

- Growing rare and protected cacti and other succulents from seed is a good way to ensure that your plants have not been collected from the wild. Propagate these plants by seed and share them with other conservation-minded growers.
- Become a member of the International Organization for Succulent Plant Study (IOS), which has been instrumental in promoting conservation (see www.iosweb.org/home.html). The IOS publishes and promotes codes of conduct for gardeners as well as collectors, importers, and nurserymen (see www.brcactaceae.org/conduct_code.html for details).
- Notify the IOS if you suspect that any supplier is violating legal controls.
- Join your local cactus and succulent society and support or help establish an active conservation committee.

Hardy Cacti: Living Sculptures of the American West

Panayoti Kelaidis

A few decades ago you would have been considered a hardy-cactus collector if you had a hedgehog cactus (*Echinocereus*) or two in your garden alongside a ball cactus (*Coryphantha vivipara* var. *vivipara*) and, of course, some prickly pears (*Opuntia*). Nowadays there are collectors in New England and the upper Midwest—even in the Pacific Northwest—who grow a hundred selections of cacti outdoors from a dozen or more genera. The explosion of interest in hardy cacti has come about because of the increasing availability of inexpensive, nursery-grown plants as well as more adventurous gardeners with improving horticultural skills.

Hardy cactus lovers no less than all succulent lovers owe an enormous debt to the dozens of nurseries in the American Southwest that have made choice succulents cheaply available from seed and eliminated the need to collect these sometimes rare plants in nature.

Growing Hardy Cacti

Hardy cacti have two key requirements: good drainage—especially in winter—and abundant sunshine. For this reason, they do best when grown among rocks. A rock garden or stone wall provide both a beautiful setting to display cacti and ensure the

Fabulous architectural plants for gardens in cold-winter regions, prickly pears and other hardy cacti reward good care with an eye-popping flower display.

Extremely cold-hardy *Hamatocactus bicolor* needs to stay dry in winter, which can be tricky in wet areas unless it is grown in a pot and moved to shelter as needed.

sharp drainage they need to grow as vigorously and sturdily as they would in nature. In the Rocky Mountain and Intermountain regions that receive less than 20 inches of precipitation annually, cacti usually grow well in heavy clay soils as well as sandier soils. In wetter regions, they are generally cultivated in a gravel and sand mixture. A slope with a generous three- to eight-inch topdressing of a gravel and sand mix provides more than enough drainage even in wet climates. This type of treatment helps to keep the vulnerable crowns dry and therefore less prone to rot and allows the cacti roots to reach down into the soil, where they find nutrients and moisture needed for good growth, especially in summer. Because these plants have evolved in dry regions where soil nutrients are not regularly leached by precipitation, if you garden in sand or gravel you may need to fertilize your cacti regularly. They will grow in lean soil, but to thrive they need nutrients. I prefer to use inorganic fertilizers such as Osmocote or Sierra Blend: usually a three-month formulation. Always err on the side of caution with succulents: They need to shut down growth in late summer and excess fertilizer can cause weak growth when frost comes.

Hardy Cacti in Containers

Hardy cacti also do well in containers, either in stone or stonelike materials such as hypertufa troughs or frost-proof stoneware containers. In a pot you can control the growing medium to provide the perfect mix for your plants. Even in dry Colorado, I use plenty of grit and some sand along with heavier loam to supply ballast and nutrients. Most succulent fanciers like to use scoria or other gravelly amendments to their favorite potting mix for succulents. The wetter the climate, the more gravel you need to add to the soil. I rarely use more than one-third scoria in my garden, but two-thirds may be too little in a rainy climate.

Many of the more moisture-sensitive Southwestern cacti, such as plains cactus (*Sclerocactus*) and fishhook cactus (*Pediocactus*), which invariably succumb when cultivated in open soil, no matter how well drained, thrive in containers.

A Collection of Hardy Cacti

Cacti are, of course, an endless source of fascination to gardeners in regions where the plants are native, and it is intriguing that they can provide so much pleasure to gardeners in cold climates that aren't traditional cactus territory. I remember seeing a large collection perched on a balcony in China. I have corresponded with enthusiasts across Europe and Asia who all want to capture a bit of the magic of the Southwestern landscape in the form of these most classic, gorgeous, and utterly defiant American wildflowers. The species below are just a few of the many plants available for growing in gardens and adaptable to a wide range of growing conditions.

Coryphantha

Hardy to –20°F, *Coryphantha vivipara* var. *vivipara* is the standout of another large genus containing many hardy plants. I grow a dozen or more selections and feel as though I have just scratched the surface. Imagine a baseball completely obscured by white or tan spines, and you have an instant image of this cactus when it's not in bloom. Some have stems that grow over eight inches in diameter, and some form

clumps that reach over a foot across in nature. The flower color varies from pale pink to deep purple-rose, and the flowers can open from May through the summer months, depending on the individual plant. There are also half a dozen subspecies from the Southwest available commercially. A miniature form of the species that is especially white-spined and petite is sometimes found throughout the range of the species. Unfortunately, it is not distinguished botanically.

Over time, **Coryphantha vivipara var. *vivipara*** produces buds that drop off and vegetatively form new plants nearby.

Claret cup cacti are a very variable group of plants: *Echinocereus triglochidiatus***, strawberry cactus, produces bright red flowers that last a few days and are followed by edible juicy red fruits.**

Just a trifle more tender are *Coryphantha sulcata* and *C. scheerii,* which can survive to –10ºF if kept dry. Both have huge bright yellow flowers.

At first glance, the tiny ball cactus *Coryphantha missouriensis* seems very much like *C. vivipara.* The strange copper flower color and brightly colored fruit will quickly distinguish it. This cactus, hardy to –25ºF, grows over much the same range as *C. vivipara,* yet is far less often found in gardens. Though not exactly showy, the straw-yellow, brown, or amber flowers are quite appealing, as are the bright red fruit that persist from late summer to spring. It is variable over its huge range and worth obtaining in various forms.

Echinocereus

The glorious hedgehog cacti with their cylindrical symmetry, like lacy columns or gothic spires, will always hold pride of place in a hardy-cactus collection. Over a dozen species have survived repeated subzero winters, and some of these include a number of subspecies and forms, so just one genus can provide a lifetime's opportunity for the hardy-cactus lover.

The main attraction among these cacti is unquestionably *Echinocereus reichenbachii,* which has the greatest cold tolerance (it is hardy to –25ºF) and is the least sensitive to excess moisture. Commonly known as lace cactus, this wonderful species is quickly and easily grown from seed and offers a tremendous range of flower color, spine development, form, and stem size. Different subspecies of lace cactus can range in size from a few inches to nearly two feet, with pure white to nearly black spines.

Fendler's hedgehog (*Echinocereus fendleri*), hardy to −20°F and almost as versatile as lace cactus, also has a number of unusual forms. The rare, corky-spined *E. fendleri* var. *kuenzleri* has become quite inexpensive in recent years and is often available. Claret cup cacti (*Echinocereus coccineus, E. polyacanthus, E. triglochidiatus*), also hardy to −20°F, occur in endless permutations, almost bewildering in their variability in nature and in cultivation. Flower color ranges from near orange, scarlet, and pink to deep crimson shades. Stems can vary from spineless to wildly tousled and reach anywhere from three inches to several feet tall, as in the White Sands form of *E. triglochidiatus* var. *gonacanthus*. Eventually, most forms can clump up to form mounds of almost mythic proportions. Studded with brilliant badminton-birdie flowers, they can stop traffic. Peak flowering comes from late April to June, depending on variety.

Among other cold-tolerant *Echinocereus* cacti is the lemon-scented *E. viridiflorus,* (−20°F), less showy but every bit as hardy as any of the species described above. A welter of hedgehog cacti generally found further south have northerly disjunct populations and high-altitude forms that are regularly subjected to subzero weather in nature and thus are hardier than other members of the species. These include *E. dasyacanthus, E. engelmanii, E. enneacanthus, E. knippelianus, E. viereckii,* and others.

Over time, many claret cup cacti, such as this scarlet hedgehog, *Echinocereus coccineus*, grow into sizable clumps that put on a spectacular flower display in late spring or early summer.

Most of these are doing fine in Denver, which lies in USDA Zone 5 (–20ºF). I wouldn't try to grow most of them in wetter regions colder than Zone 7, however, unless they could be kept in an unusually protected microclimate with ideal soil conditions. Seek out the most cold-tolerant cultivar for testing. Larger plants tend to survive the first winter better than tiny seedlings. If you have small seedlings or plants, I recommend leaving them in the seed pot rather than planting them out too early.

Escobaria

Quite a few species in the genus *Escobaria*, which is closely related to *Mammillaria*, have proven themselves in a wide range of climates. *Escobaria sneedii* var. *leei*, hardy to –20ºF, is one of our tiniest and rarest cacti, restricted in nature to the Carlsbad Cavern area in Texas. In cultivation it thrives almost everywhere in North America, in places as diverse as New England rock gardens and troughs in Colorado. It makes a huddled mound of marble-size stems densely covered in white-spines, with pale pink flowers in early summer. *Escobaria sneedii* var. *sneedii*, hardy to –15ºF, is similar in form but larger and with pinker flowers. Larger still is *E. organensis*, hardy to –15ºF. The largest relative is *E. orcuttii*, hardy to –15ºF, from the mountains of southern New Mexico and yet extremely hardy far northward. These are all rather small plants, rarely more than a foot at the very biggest—either in height or spread. *Escobaria hesteri* and *E. minima*, which resemble dwarf races of *Corypantha vivipara*, can survive to –10ºF in dry-winter regions.

Maihuenia poepiggii

Surprisingly, this prickly pear cousin with cylindrical stems and persistent tubular true leaves has grown vigorously for many years in gardens throughout the Pacific Northwest, where it is the best-performing outdoor cactus. It even blooms prolifically there, producing luminous, two-inch pale yellow roselike flowers. It is hardy to –15ºF and can survive even colder temperatures in the interior West.

Opuntia, Cylindropuntia, and Grusonia

The endless variations of prickly pear, cholla, and creeping cylindrical opuntia are the glory and bane of the hardy-cactus garden: Few plants combine such brilliant flowers and architectural stems and forms with such painful spines and glochids (spines that come off easily). The secret for growing *Opuntia* and closely allied genera is siting them where they won't need constant care. I prefer to grow them primarily in

A common sight in the Southwest, some chollas take a shrublike form, like these wild-growing specimens; other species grow to tree size or creep along the ground.

large pots, where they droop gracefully and are easily weeded and maintained. Strategically positioned among rocks, they can likewise be managed for years without the need for cleanup and cutting back that can cause gardeners such discomfort. And opuntias are so easily propagated by severing and planting a pad, or even part of a pad, that there is no excuse for not quickly building a wonderful collection.

Scattered over the eastern two-thirds of the United States and a short way into Canada, *Opuntia humifusa* may be the most widely distributed prickly pear. It is certainly the most widely cultivated. Most forms are nearly spineless, and even its glochids are less lethal than those of most western prickly pears. In summer, the bright green mass of stems provides a fine contrast to the predominant silvers and grays of other cacti, but in winter it wilts into a limp mass of darkened matter aptly described as "depressa." In spring, it resurrects miraculously within weeks of the return of warm weather. It can be dazzling in early summer, when it is intermittently covered with bright yellow flowers. Despite its wide range, there have been surprisingly few selections: *O. humifusa* 'Lemon Spreader' is one of the few cultivars. The closely related *O. macrorrhiza* of the southern Rockies seems to be much more variable in both pad shape and flower color. As with so many cacti, the potential for hybridization is limitless.

Over much of the 20th century, some of the finest *Opuntia* selections were made by Claude Barr, the great nurseryman of the Great Plains: His clones *Opuntia* 'Crystal Tide' (−25ºF), 'Claude Arno' (−25ºF), and others still form the basis of many hardy cactus gardens. These are mostly hybrids of *O. polyacantha*, the commonest cactus in the West.

Opuntia fragilis (–35oF) has the honor of being the most northerly cactus, growing hundreds of miles north of the Canada-U.S. border. It has provided many fascinating selections, including nearly spineless forms with spherical pads and bright bright pink or yellow flowers produced quite generously. Hunger cactus (*O. polyacantha*, hardy to –25oF) must be the most abundant western species, with flowers in every imaginable shade of

With abundant sunshine and good drainage, especially in winter, hardy cacti do well in most areas of North America. The cholla cactus shown here braves winter in a Connecticut garden.

yellow to pink and deep red. *Opuntia phaeacantha* (hardy to –20oF) is nearly as variable, with statuesque pads, especially in the tall variety (*O. engelmannii*, hardy to –15oF). It is not unheard of to find these up to six feet tall.

Few plants are as statuesque as *Cylindropuntia imbricata* (hardy to –15oF) and its many cousins: *C. echinocarpa* (–15oF), *C. kleiniae* (–20oF), *C. leptocaulis* (–20oF), and *C. spinosior* (–15oF). These form tall, almost treelike candelabra with midsummer flowers and showy autumnal seedpods.

The creeping cylindrical opuntias of the Southwest have had a botanical name change and are now called *Grusonia*. The hardiest of these is undoubtedly *G. clavata* (–25oF), with wide, bright white sheathlike spines and a dense, creeping habit that is as appealing as the two-inch pale yellow flowers. In nature, this plant can spread many feet across: Gardeners are pleased if it spreads to a foot after many years, however.

Pediocactus and *Sclerocactus*

Plants of high, cold, dry mountain ridges or hot deserts, most species of plains cactus and fishhook cactus grow in regions where subzero cold is a frequent winter phenomenon, making them endlessly teasing to gardeners in cold climates. They are useful in dry-region gardens where gardeners control their impulse to water, but they are only apt to gain wide currency in wet regions if and when they can be obtained grafted onto moisture-tolerant rootstocks, such as *Opuntia fragilis* or perhaps *Coryphantha vivipara*. Though grafted

Cacti and other succulents thrive in the humid summers of the Northeast, as they mingle with perennials in the Connecticut garden of John Spain.

plants are rarely available, you can perhaps do the grafting yourself—it's not as hard as you might imagine. (For a few tips, see "Propagating Cacti and Succulents," page 80.)

More Cacti

Quite a few unusual ball cacti have gained wide currency, although they are more challenging in wetter regions: *Echinocactus texensis, Echinomastus intertextus, Epithelantha micromeris, Hamatocactus bicolor,* and *Mammillaria wrightii* all have cold-hardy variants that can survive subzero cold provided they stay dry. Gardeners in the interior West have brought a surprising range of South American cacti through many winters, including *Echinopsis* (often sold and listed in catalogs as *Lobivia*), *Gymnocalycium, Parodia* (often sold and listed as *Notocactus*), as well as numerous opuntioids such as *Maihueniopsis, Puna,* and *Tephrocacti,* which are all subject to extreme cold in the Andes. There is now such a wealth of data available on many South American cacti that I expect they will be a large new basis for experimentation in the coming decades.

Hardy Succulents: Drought-Tolerant Beauties for All Regions

Panayoti Kelaidis

Who can resist growing succulents now that such a lavish smorgasbord of species is available, suitable even for the coldest parts of North America? Succulents figure prominently in container gardens and in traditional perennial borders. They are key elements in xeriscape gardens, a term that can cover a number of styles but generally denotes an informal perennial garden modeled on a dry western landscape, usually sited on somewhat harsh, mineral soil or in an exposed spot. They have also found their place in rock gardens, where they grow (and look) better than temperamental alpines. After all, what grander rock gardens are there in nature than the Grand Canyon and the wild, rocky landscapes of the American Southwest, which are creeping and crawling with succulents?

Most gardeners associate succulents with drought, and it is true that a particularly large number of species occur naturally in deserts and steppe regions and need special care when grown in humid, maritime climates. Most hardy succulents thrive among rocks and are ideal denizens of rock gardens. Well-drained soil on a sunny, exposed slope or crevice amended with sand or gravel and left to dry out between waterings can make all the difference in their success. Many succulents benefit from

A boon for a sunny garden in any region, drought-tolerant succulents like the mat-forming, yellow-flowered *Delosperma* and sword-leafed *Yucca* thrive with minimal care once they are established in well-draining soil.

A member of a large genus of mat-forming or clumping succulents in the ice plant family, *Delosperma cooperi* produces a wealth of bright flowers all summer long.

protection from excessive rain—a site under an overhang or a pane of glass overhead during torrential rains may suffice to make them happy. Succulents have a much easier time getting through the colder months if they get a chance to dry out as much as possible before winter sets in: Drying out helps to enhance their hardiness, which seems to improve as they mature. But there are succulents that grow in moist habitats as well, such as species in the *Hylotelephium* group of *Sedum*, which do best with loamy soils and regular watering. There are also a few species of *Crassula* and *Rhodiola* that can grow near streams or even with their feet permanently wet.

It's also worth noting that succulents are among the easiest plants to propagate: Removing a small offset and putting it where you want a new plant to grow is all it takes for many of them, including sedums and sempervivums.

Hardy Succulents in Containers

There are few more striking ways to display succulents outdoors than in elegant, harmonizing containers. Any succulent that is reliably cold hardy in your climate can likely survive the winter in a container. You may be surprised to find, as I have been, that some succulents actually do better in shallow pots than in the ground. In nature, *Orostachys*, for instance, almost always grows in the shallowest of soils on rocks, preferring conditions often easier to approximate in a pot than in the ground. Rangier succulents, like sedums, are more easily controlled in a container, where they are less likely to spread into their neighbors' territory or be overtaken by weeds. Pots have to be sufficiently large—at least ten inches in diameter—and frost-resistant.

I have found that succulents need sustenance as well as drainage: In Colorado I use a good garden loam for half the volume of soil mix. In wetter climates you may use less to improve drainage. I do find a gravel mulch helps keep the pot from drying too quickly until the succulents are established. After the first year, a light application of a good slow-release fertilizer like Osmocote or Sierra Blend is helpful once a year. Just scatter a few teaspoons on the soil surface in spring.

A Selection of Hardy Succulents for Every Garden

The majority of succulents in both North and South America, and also in Africa, come from deserts where it never freezes, or where frost is a fleeting phenomenon. Gardeners in Zone 8 or warmer (minimum winter temperature in the 20°F range) have a wealth of species to choose from, but gardeners in subzero winter areas are catching up fast: Almost every year it seems that dozens of very cold-hardy succulents become widely available, greatly expanding the palette of succulents that can survive and even thrive in regions with subzero winters.

Delosperma

Just 20 years ago, few gardeners would have believed that there soon would be dozens of South African succulents making their homes in the colder parts of North America. The best-known South African succulents are the endless varieties of *Delosperma,* one of the largest and most widespread genera in the ice plant family (Aizoaceae). The plants superficially resemble sedums but are generally even more fleshy and tend to make even denser, weed-suppressing mats. The flowers often completely obscure the foliage in late spring, sometimes with repeated flushes right to fall.

The first *Delosperma* to gain wide currency was *D. nubigenum* 'Lesotho' (hardy to −20°F), which covers itself with yellow daisylike flowers in spring. This is likely a sterile hybrid, as it has never been known to produce seed. It has been successfully grown into Zone 4 (−20°F), especially in drier areas of the country. *Delosperma cooperi* (−15°F) was introduced in the mid-1980s and has become a garden mainstay all over America. It produces plush, dark blue-green mats with an almost constant succession of bright purple-magenta two-inch flowers all summer. It is reliably hardy only in Zone 6 and warmer, but it grows well in Zone 5 in drier parts of the West. Higher-altitude forms have recently been introduced that promise much greater cold tolerance, and the first hybrids are emerging: *Delosperma* 'Kelaidis' (or MESA VERDE; –25°F) appears to be a cross between a yellow and a pink species: Its iridescent flowers are salmon pink with hints of orange—unique and striking. *Delosperma basuticum* 'Gold Nugget' (–30°F) is clump-forming and produces two-inch yellow flowers with a white eye in very early spring. It has overwintered in Calgary, Canada, and at 8,000 feet in the Colorado Rockies. Another stunning *Delosperma* was described by science only after it had been propagated and distributed in America under an incorrect name: *Delosperma sphalmanthoides* (–15°F), as it is correctly called, forms dense clumps of tubular, blue-tufted foliage that is completely obscured in early spring by shining pink flowers. It is extremely restricted in its range in the Komsberg region of the high Karoo of South Africa, and I am quite sure there are more plants in cultivation in North America today than are growing in all its wild habitat.

Over a hundred genera in the ice plant family have overwintered at least one year in Zone 5 (–20°F) Denver, Colorado. I obtained most of these from mail-order nurseries, where they have been grown for decades as houseplants, including many species of *Aloinopsis, Bergeranthus, Chasmatophyllum, Drosanthemum, Hereroa, Malephora, Nananthus, Stomatium,* and *Titanopsis.* Most of these are from the Karoo and need protection from winter wet in humid climates, but many have made it through sub-zero winters as far north as New York City (–10°F).

Many ice plants are challenging to grow in wetter climates, but many others thrive in humid regions: The latter all hail from South Africa's Drakensberg Mountains, which receive more than 60 inches of rain a year. There are perhaps even more hardy succulents to be found in the East Cape Mountains a bit further to the west and south, an area that is fiercely cold because of its greater latitude. *Anacampseros rufescens, Aloe ecklonis, Cotyledon orbiculata, Crassula sarcocaulis,* and *Othonna capensis* are proving hardy in Zone 5 (–20°F) in the arid western U.S., but they are more likely to successfully overwinter in Zone 7 (0°F) or warmer on the wetter eastern seaboard. A few species of the family, in particular members of the genus *Carpobrotus,* have proven to be noxious weeds in coastal California. *Delosperma* are much smaller and pose far less of a threat for invasiveness, but gardeners should always exercise vigilance lest one of our garden beauties pose a menace to natural environments.

Bright flowers rise high above the ground-hugging foliage of lewisias. Though not yet listed as endangered, these North American natives are threatened by wild collection—as are most plants in this book.

Lewisia

Some of the loveliest hardy succulents grow wild right across North America. Lewisias have been an object of great interest among rock gardeners for much of the 20th century and into the 21st, but in the last two decades, selections have become available that grow more easily in a wide range of garden conditions. They are sometimes sold inexpensively by garden centers much like bedding plants, but they will perennialize easily with proper treatment. Best known are the brilliant-colored forms of *Lewisia cotyledon* (hardy to –20ºF), whose flowers range from white and yellow through all the bright hard-candy shades of purple, pink, and orange. A bed of these in full bloom creates a spectacle not soon forgotten. The rare and even showier yellow- to apricot-colored *L. tweedyi* (–25ºF) also seems to be showing up in more and more gardens. Interestingly, thanks to tissue culture, a great number of hybrids, such as 'Trevosia', 'Little Plum', and 'Edithae' are appearing in garden centers. They seem to better tolerate overwatering and also rebloom more through the summer.

Orostachys and Rosularia

Closely allied to *Sedum*, *Orostachys* and *Rosularia* have gained far wider currency in recent years. Both form symmetrical rosettes that superficially resemble *Sempervivum*. *Orostachys* species occur primarily in eastern Asia, where they can be found perching on cliffs, steep, rocky shorelines, and roofs. They generally bloom in fall, forming pagodalike spikes of chartreuse or cream flowers. The rosettes of most species curl up into tight balls in winter, offering great seasonal interest.

Several enchanting miniatures, rarely more than half a foot tall even in bloom, have been introduced recently from China: *Orostachys chanetii* from Lushan, with bright pink flowers, the brown-stained *O. fimbriata* from Suzhou, and almost tropical-colored amber and maroon *O. erubescens*. Alas, these are generally not hardy below 0°F unless kept very dry in winter. They usually do not come into full bloom until after the first heavy frost, which mars their flowers. Definitely a tough one, *Orostachys spinosa* ventures inland deep into Siberia, where it has been subjected to temperatures below −60°F. This statuesque succulent always piques interest, forming a steel-gray rosette resembling a very compact, stylized artichoke and eventually producing a picturesque spire of bloom in summer, like a platinum pagoda.

Rosularia species are found from the Mediterranean to the Himalaya, mostly concentrated in the high, dry mountains of western Asia. These look like nothing so much as rather hairy or extravagant hens and chicks, only with very beautiful spires of bloom in a wide array of colors. The species range from the yellow-flowered *R. aizoon* (−15°F) and *R. chrysantha* (−20°F) to bright pink or white *R. sempervivum* (−20°F) and every variation in between. Half a dozen species have gained relatively wide currency in recent years, further widening the horizons of succulent enthusiasts in cold climates.

Phemeranthus (syn. *Talinum*)

The genus *Phemeranthus* (syn. *Talinum*) was once almost unknown in gardens, and to make matters worse, those that made it into catalogs and nurseries were—and still are—often listed as in the genus *Talinum*. Numerous native species have come into cultivation lately, including the brilliant pink, everblooming form of *Phemeranthus calycinus* from the Ozarks that self-sows widely in many gardens. This species resembles a sprightly sedum with attenuated leaves and stems possessing a ballerinalike grace. The threadlike stems up to a foot in height boast pirouettes of waxy hot-pink flowers for months on end. It has proven hardy to −25°F. Two miniature species from the Pacific Northwest—tiny spreading to ascending white-flowered *P. sediformis* and taller, clump-forming *P. spinescens*, with pink flowers on five-inch stems—are likewise hardy to −25°F as long as they are not wet in winter. Large-flowered cousins from the Southwest like *P. brevicaulis* and *P. brevifolius*, among others, provide a similar long

Extremely unfussy, hardy succulents like mat-forming *Sedum spurium* make wonderful rock garden plants.

season of showy bloom above more compact mats and clumps. Most all of these are hardy well below –10°F (if protected from too much wetness in winter).

Sedum

Novel species and selections of *Sedum* from China, Europe, and the American West are practically flooding the market. None of the plants chosen here spread aggressively, and all are permanent, welcome additions to the garden. *Sedum pachyclados* (hardy to –25°F) is an especially beautiful and restrained species with silvery, toothed leaves and creamy-white flowers. Introduced from Pakistan, it is now widely grown. The foliage of *S. rupestre* 'Angelina' (–20°F) is fine-textured and Day-Glo chartreuse bordering on orange in sun or shade. This sedum makes a striking accent plant and works beautifully as edging or draped gracefully over stonework. *Sedum spurium* 'John Creech' (–25°F) makes dense, miniature mats of neatly scalloped dark green rosettes barely an inch across in shade or sun. *Sedum takesimense* (–15°F) is a robust clump-forming, yellow-flowering species from an island in the Sea of Japan. *Sedum tetractinum* (–15°F), from China, has lustrous, army-green foliage that forms a dense mat with sparkling yellow flowers—very distinct from other species.

Dozens of cultivars of *Sedum spectabile* (–30°F) are available in a wide range of colors from white-flowered 'Stardust' to 'Neon', a vibrant pink-flowered cultivar, to purple-leafed 'Mohrchen' and maroon-stemmed 'Matrona.' Many of the recent cultivars have originated in Germany, but Great Britain also produces many classics, like the very showy 'Vera Jameson' with lustrous blue-green, purple-stained mounds of foliage and a long season of bright rose flowers.

Woody Lilies: *Dasylirion*, *Hesperaloe*, *Nolina*, and *Yucca*

The woody lilies, as they are sometimes called, have become important landscape plants not just in the desert Southwest but far northward as gardeners have discovered that they are much more cold-tolerant than their native range might indicate. These imposing succulents can transform even the most conventional suburban landscape into a magical outpost of the Southwestern desert. Their bold rosettes of foliage and spectacular blooms (so distinct in each species) must be sited with some care in the garden. They provide stunning focal points that garden designers have come to value and use quite lavishly. And who can resist the gigantic white candelabra flowers when they finally emerge?

Dasylirion is the most tender of these four classic Southwestern genera. *Dasylirion wheeleri* (hardy to –10ºF) extends as far as south-central New Mexico, but even plants from the northernmost reaches of its range sustain some frost damage in Denver when they are young. Here it is best to postpone planting them in the ground until they have graduated to gallon-size pots at least. Consider mulching lightly with crisp leaves (like oak) or pine needles in their first winters in the ground. The giant rosettes, with vicious marginal spines that point in two directions, require careful placement. After many years, the giant flower stalks shoot up to ten or more feet, terminating in a glorious, shaggy yellow inflorescence that quickly transforms into imposing, long-lasting stiff seed heads. *Dasylirion texanum* (–20ºF) comes from the Texas hill country, farther south and east than *D. wheeleri.* It appears to tolerate greater cold and moisture than its more northerly cousin. Go figure.

Hesperaloe parviflora, restricted to Mexico and the lower Rio Grande Valley in Texas in nature, has proven indestructible in Zone 5 winters in dry regions, and to at least Zone 6 in moister climates. Its sturdy clumps of dark green, threadlike foliage are attractive in their own right, but the tall wands of coral red or even yellow lily-like flowers through the summer months make an enchanting picture in any garden.

From a distance, *Nolina* superficially resembles a dense clump of lush, evergreen grass. Even in the depths of winter, however, it keeps its lush, dark green color and makes a wonderful statement in the garden. The hardiest species is undoubtedly *N. texana* (hardy to –25ºF), particularly if you can obtain it from a nursery that propagates plants from the more northerly distribution in Colorado and Oklahoma.

Unfortunately, the ivory clusters of flowers in this species are produced deep among the leaves and make a less impressive show than the other, more tender species. *Nolina microcarpa* (–15°F) is a very striking plant with very variable flower-stem size and habit. Its clouds of showy, ivory-colored flowers can reach upwards of eight feet on well-established specimens, making a great show in the garden. Some nurseries indicate where the seed originated: Always look for plants from their more northerly distribution: New Mexico or northern Texas are the best.

Yuccas appear to be even hardier, especially *Yucca glauca, Y. harrimaniae,* and *Y. baccata.* The first two species both have narrow, gray foliage, but *Y. glauca* is generally much larger than its cousin of the Intermountain region. There are many tiny forms of *Y. harrimaniae* with foliage clumps sometimes less than eight inches in diameter. Though not universally recognized in horticultural literature, these forms might be offered with distinct names, such as *Y. nana* (Hochstaetter) or *Y. sterilis.* They are extremely attractive in the garden. These have been called dollhouse yuccas and are eagerly sought by hardy-succulent lovers. Conversely, *Y. baccata* grows to immense dimensions: Rosettes seven feet across are not unheard of. The foliage can be deep green and quite wide, and the plant is sometimes confused with agaves by neophytes. *Yucca baccata* has survived many years in gardens where temperatures drop below –20°F. Surprisingly, many of the giant Chihuahuan species that can attain almost treelike proportions, such as *Yucca faxoniana, Y. rostrata,* and *Y. thompsoniana,* have weathered repeated subzero temperatures in Denver with virtually no frost damage.

Slow-growing *Hesperaloe parviflora* forms a sturdy clump of evergreen foliage that reaches about three feet tall and spreads to six feet.

Medicinal Cacti and Succulents: Powerful Plants for Windowsills, Light Carts, and Backyards

Stephen Maciejewski

Last time I checked, my medicine cabinet contained bottles of *Aloe vera*, *Echinacea*, *Panax ginseng*, *Ginkgo biloba*, *Paullinia cupana* (guarana), and *Hoodia gordonii*, all picked up from the shelves of health-food stores stacked with a much wider assortment of plant-derived medicines and supplements. Of the substantial number of medicines coming directly from the plant world, some are so common that we take them for granted: Consider a tried-and-true botanical like aspirin, originally derived from the bark of willows, now generated from synthetic sources; or quinine, from the bark of *Cinchona* tree species, used to treat malaria; or the painkiller morphine, an alkaloid derived from the opium poppy, *Papaver somniferum*.

The field of ethnobotany is expanding at an enormous rate, and many promising plants—cacti and other succulents among them—are being investigated for their medicinal potential or have already found their way into pharmacies and our homes. The common succulent *Aloe vera*, for example, produces sap effective in treating burns, and the plant is often kept on hand in backyard gardens and on windowsills.

The stunning bulb of *Bowiea volubilis* gives rise to a single vine that wraps itself around any support it is offered. It keeps growing until fall, when it turns brown and drops off as the plant goes dormant.

In regions with serious frost, *Agave parryi* must be moved indoors in winter. Elsewhere it makes a striking year-round garden plant that is unattractive to deer.

Commercially, the sap is a popular ingredient in sunburn creams and gels and treatments for chapped hands and lips. Lots of folks grow *Sempervivum*, the houseleek. Did you know that it has been used over the centuries to relieve various skin ailments?

Tapping the healing powers of cacti and other succulents is not just a modern pursuit. For millennia, indigenous peoples worldwide have used them to treat a variety of health problems. Among the cacti employed for their medicinal properties are *Ariocarpus, Astrophytum, Aztekium, Cylindropuntia, Echinocereus, Echinopsis, Epithelantha, Escobaria, Grusonia, Lophophora, Mammillaria, Obregonia, Opuntia, Pachycereus, Peniocereus, Selenicereus, Trichocereus,* and *Turbinicarpus*. Some useful succulents are *Agave, Aloe, Avonia, Boswellia, Bowiea, Bursera, Commiphora, Dioscorea, Haworthia, Hoodia gordonii* (see page 54 for more information on this plant), and *Sempervivum*.

Today, medicinal plants are big business. It is estimated that in South Africa alone 20,000 tons of plant materials are traded each year, and a good percentage of these plants are succulents collected in the wild. Unfortunately, with increasing population densities and rapid urbanization, enormous pressures are placed on the natural habitats of these plants. Records show that plant gatherers need to go farther and farther afield to collect them. Until these plants are protected in their natural habitats and successfully farmed, many are doomed to eradication from the wild.

Medicinal Plants to Grow at Home

Whether antiseptic or antibiotic, hallucinogenic, diuretic, or cure-all, medicinal cacti and succulents are a fascinating group. I grow a number of them because I'm attracted to the stories behind the plants. I wonder about the adventurers who came to discover the beneficial properties of certain plants. I'm curious about how they collected (or stumbled across), prepared, and used medicinal plants. The information I gather provides me with a sort of handle on the plants, a way of getting to know another side of them. Attraction is not just skin deep, though. It is their natural history and the link between the plants and humans that helps me to better appreciate them.

Unless noted otherwise, all of the medicinal plants that follow benefit from a summer spent outside and should be moved into the house as temperatures drop in fall to avoid winter freeze in colder areas.

Agave parryi

The broad, bluish-gray-green leaves of this strikingly beautiful plant are shaped like spears and tipped with a potentially dangerous, sharp black spine. Sometimes called Parry's agave or mescal agave, this native of the Sonoran and Chihuahuan deserts of southwestern North America ranges from Arizona to New Mexico and south into Mexico, where it grows on dry, rocky slopes. In its native environment it can reach a height of two feet and grow to four feet in diameter. The plant is used for food, fiber, soap, weapons, and medicine. The sap is antiseptic, diuretic, and has laxative properties. The Aztecs drank the sap straight; the Tarahumara people cooked it to make mescal; and the Havasupai mixed baked agave buds with water to produce wine. Today, distilled products called mezcal or tequila (produced in the region of Tequila, Mexico) are widely available. This sun-loving plant should spend the winter on a light cart close to the lights or on a sunny windowsill waiting to be summered outside.

Aloe ferox

This stunning plant is sometimes referred to as the grandfather of all aloes. When young it has bluish-green leaves, which are covered with toothlike spines. At maturity, it can reach 15 feet in height with a rosette of dull green to reddish-green leaves. It retains its dried lower leaves, which make it look as if it were wearing a petticoat. Native to South Africa, this single-stem aloe grows in a wide range of habitats and is common on rocky hillsides.

The leaves and roots are boiled in water to prepare a laxative. The entire plant can be utilized to treat a number of ailments, including arthritis, conjunctivitis, eczema, hypertension, and stress. The bitter yellow juice from just below the skin is also collected and dried to make a powder that is used for a variety of problems. About half a gram works as a laxative, and a quarter gram is the dose used to treat arthritis. Externally, it is useful as an aid in treating sores and wounds.

Don't be put off by this plant's mature size—it takes a long time to get there. Acquire a young plant and enjoy its barbaric adolescent look, since the scary-looking spines become less obvious with age. *Aloe ferox* is another plant that responds well to spending the summer outdoors before being moved inside for a few months under lights or on a bright windowsill.

Aloe vera

This plant is primarily known for its healing properties, hence its telltale common names: medicine plant, immortality plant, and more recently, burn plant. *Aloe vera* has short stems and leaves up to 20 inches in length. It is suckering and forms dense groups in its native habitat in the Canary and Cape Verde islands, off the northwest coast Africa.

Many people are familiar with this plant and the products that are made with it. The sap is used extensively to treat burns, cuts, and a variety of skin ailments. Just take off a bottom leaf and rub the mucilaginous sap over the afflicted area. It reduces inflammation, swelling, and redness and protectively coats the area, speeding up the healing process. To maintain freshness, freeze any remaining leaf portion. The sap is also used to treat insect bites and poison ivy. Some people peel off the bitter green

skin and extract the gel—a clear jellylike substance—to make a beverage for boosting the immune system. *Aloe vera* sap has also been reported to help with blood-sugar regulation, osteoarthritis, colitis, and peptic ulcers.

Aloe vera prefers well-drained soils and is widely naturalized in temperate areas. It also makes a great houseplant and can be summered outside.

Aloe vera is now a popular home remedy, and its pointy leaves are often available at grocery stores and farmers' markets.

Barely rising above the soil surface, *Ariocarpus fissuratus* hides a long taproot that needs a deep pot to accommodate it comfortably.

Ariocarpus fissuratus

This piece of living sculpture grows so low to the ground that it is sometimes partially submerged, earning the name living rock. To appreciate the beauty of this tough, wrinkled plant, picture a flat rosette of triangular, spineless, rough-surfaced tubercles with a tight woolly crown. In its natural habitat on rocky, barren slopes in northern Mexico and southern Texas, it is a widespread, highly variable species that can reach a diameter of six inches. *Ariocarpus fissuratus* has been used externally as a painkiller for wounds, snakebites, and bruises. The juice has been imbibed an aid in the treatment of fever and for rheumatism. The plant can be mixed with water, boiled, and made into an intoxicating beverage. It has also been reported that long-distance runners have made use of its stimulating qualities by chewing on the tubercles.

This favorite plant, nestled in a clay pot, gets a dry winter's rest. I always have it perched on top of an inverted pot, placed right in the center of the light cart just below the tubes. It's bright and hot there, so every now and then I'll mist it.

Ariocarpus retusus

Ariocarpus retusus is another slow-growing living sculpture that can almost disappear into the ground. The tubercles are usually gray-green, sometimes a darker green. They range in shape from broad and short with an angled keel to more angular and long—like *A. fissuratus*, this species exhibits lots of variability. Given enough time and favorable conditions it can reach 12 inches in diameter. It is common and widespread throughout the Chihuahuan Desert, where it is still used at native tribal ceremonies and harvest festivals. The Huichol Indians of Mexico consider the plant too dangerous to eat and classify it as false peyote; some say it can even cause insanity. Nevertheless, it has been used in the treatment of fevers. This plant spends the winter months inside, close to the lights on a cart.

Avonia papyracea

Think of a pot of bird droppings, a collection of mealy bugs on steroids, or a mass of feathery maggots, and you might better imagine the look of this plant, which can actually be very cute. What it lacks in size—given enough time it can grow into a four- to five-inch clump—it makes up for in texture, shape, and color. Many half-inch-thick, close-scaled white stems that look like baby fingers crown this tiny, tuberous-rooted succulent. Paper-thin white scales protect the plant from predators and the intense sun of its harsh native habitat, the hot quartz deserts of Namibia and South Africa.

This plant has been used as a fermenting agent for making mead. It has also been reported to have psychoactive properties. This little gem thrives on heat. Place it as close as possible to the fluorescent tubes on a inverted pot, so close that it is not only bathed in light but can also feel the heat.

Boswellia carteri

Strange, bizarre, twisted, and contorted—all these descriptions are accurate for the shape this plant develops in its harsh environment. Although it still can reach a height of 25 feet in the wild, the severe conditions of its native environment in Somalia often sculpt this succulent tree into natural bonsai. The dried sap collected from the tree—called frankincense, or more poetically, dried tears—has been widely sought after since the beginnings of recorded history for use in incense, perfumes, embalming, cosmetics, and medicine. It has been used internally as a stimulant and topically for treatment of rheumatism, wounds, and athletic injuries. It has anti-inflammatory, antiseptic, antibacterial, and antifungal properties. Give the plant as much light as you can in your home.

Bowiea volubilis

Succulent enthusiasts love this plant. It looks like a globe of green jade resting on the ground, sometimes camouflaged by a paper-thin, brownish covering resembling onion skins (which was removed from the specimen shown on page 34). The spherical aboveground bulb can grow to a foot in diameter. It has a slender, branched, leafless green vine growing out of the top that reaches up to 15 feet in length. Native to the eastern provinces of South Africa and Mozambique, it is commonly known as climbing onion and sometimes referred to as Zulu potato. This plant can be very dangerous to ingest, as it contains a number of cardiac glycosides that are 30 times stronger than digitalis. Herbalists use the bulb and bulb scales to treat a variety of ailments, including headaches, bladder problems, and female infertility. Figures for 1998 show that 43 tons of *Bowiea volubilis* were collected from the wild and sold by rural gatherers, street traders, shops, and healers; this amounts to about 386,000 bulbs.

This plant goes dormant in winter. When the green vine turns brown, it's time to stop watering. Let it rest. When a new green shoot appears from the center of the bulb, give it a drink. You can let the vine grow up a trellis or trail down over the edge of its pot, or you can train it over and around a frame, easily made from two wires bent in half with both ends inserted into the pot and crossing each other at the top (see page 34).

Bursera fagaroides

This shrub or small tree has it all: The tight, smooth, reddish-brown to gray bark peels back to reveal gray-green tones. The aromatic leaves give off a citrus odor when crushed. The sap is the source of copal, a highly aromatic, sweet citrus-scented resin. Its very short and thick trunk also makes it a natural bonsai when potted, although in its native habitat it can reach a height of 16 feet and is wide spreading. It grows

Reaching treelike proportions in its native habitat in the Chihuahuan and Sonoran deserts, *Bursera fagaroides* stays small when grown in a pot.

throughout the Sonoran and Chihuahuan deserts. The ancient Maya and Aztecs used the resin of this plant for incense offerings to the gods, and their descendants still use it today in protection and purification ceremonies. Dried chunks of the sap are also collected, powdered, and then dissolved in alcohol or vegetable oils to access their superior antiseptic properties.

Container-grown specimens will stay small and manageable. Although they can go through a dormant period and lose most of their leaves, they will still retain their attractive rugged look. *Bursera fagaroides* is perfect for a sunny winter windowsill.

Dioscorea mexicana (syn. *D. macrostachya*)

You can't help but admire the sculptural artistry of this vining plant, which is native to southern Mexico and Guatemala. It develops a huge caudex (enlarged stem), giving it the name turtleback plant or Mexican tortoise shell yam. With time, it can reach a height of two feet with a very impressive three-foot spread. It has large, shiny, heart-shaped leaves tapering to a point, with heavy venation. The Aztecs called it the "graceful plant" and used it for their skin. North American native peoples have also used this plant to treat problems of the reproductive system. The tubers are rich in diosgenin, a plant steroid, and were once used in the preparation of contraceptive pills. Due to overcollecting, the turtleback plant was nearly eradicated in the wild during the search for commercially valuable sources of hormonal substances. Fortunately, collection pressure on the plant eased once synthetic substances were developed in 1970.

Dioscorea mexicana grows in sun or part shade and prefers warm but not hot weather. It drops its leaves during dormancy (as shown on page 77), during which it should be moderately watered to keep it from drying out completely.

Haworthia limifolia

Nicknamed the fairy washboard because of the distinct, perfectly spaced ridges on its tough, dry, green leaves, *Haworthia limifolia* forms clustering, stemless rosettes up to eight inches wide. The succulent is native to Mozambique, Swaziland, and South Africa's Gauteng (formerly Transvaal) and Kwazulu-Natal provinces, growing on east-facing slopes in well-drained, rocky soils. It is used by the Zulu to treat gastrointestinal problems and is prized by traditional African healers. During 1998, in just one area of Africa, 22.5 tons of plant material were traded, amounting to about 479,000 plants.

Haworthia limifolia is becoming uncommon in its native range but has become a common plant in collections. It is easy to grow, preferring partial to full shade. Water it regularly in summer, but keep it on the drier side in winter.

Obregonia denegrii

This monotypic (only one species in the genus) cactus is sometimes called the artichoke cactus for its shape; others say it looks like a green pinecone. Whatever the common name, it is a joy to behold. It grows in a symmetrical whorl of green incurved tubercles—in essence a ball of wedgelike stems—crowned with a furry white tassel. It can grow to nearly eight inches in diameter. It is native to the valley of Jaumave, in the state of Tamaulipas, Mexico. Unfortunately, it is now listed as Vulnerable on the international Red List of Threatened Species. The wild population has dramatically decreased by 50 percent, and as of 2002, there were only about 5,000 individual plants left in the wild. The primary threats have been erosion, livestock grazing, illegal commercial collection, and collection by locals for medicinal purposes. These plants have been used in the treatment of rheumatism and have antibiotic qualities. They also contain alkaloids similar to those found in peyote but in insignificant amounts. Surprisingly, this species does not need direct sun to grow well.

It's best to keep *Obregonia denegrii* dry when watering to avoid damaging the tuft of "wool" in the plant's center, which will later give rise to a day-blooming white flower.

Ceropegias: Fabulous Vines of the Succulent World

Sage Reynolds

I saw my first photograph of a ceropegia when I was about ten years old. It was *Ceropegia racemosa* subspecies *setifera*, and I was struck by the unusual flower and its graphic coloring. This was a plant I wanted to grow. However, it wasn't until about 30 years later, in the late 1980s, that I was able to find and begin to grow these vines with their weirdly sculptural and colorful flowers.

Ceropegias are plants of tropical and subtropical regions from the Canary Islands (where *Ceropegia fusca* is native) through Africa and Madagascar to China, Indonesia, and northern Australia. They are found in a wide range of habitats from equatorial forest to semidesert.

The wide climatic and geographical range gives rise to a variety of plant shapes and habits. Most ceropegias are vines—including all that are discussed in this article—but there are some that resemble small bushes, stands of gray organ pipes (*Ceropegia fusca*), slithering snakes (*C. stapeliiformis*), and legless lizards (*C. armandii*). The stems can be as thick as cigars (*C. stapeliiformis*) or as thin as twine (*C. ampliata, C. leroyi*). The leaves usually appear in pairs opposite each other, at nodes along the stems. The leaves can be minuscule (*C. stapeliiformis*), very succulent (*C. sandersonii*), paper thin and deciduous (*C. elegans*), large and broad (*C. cumingiana*), needlelike (*C. dichotoma*), or absent (*C. devecchii*). The roots of some ceropegias are fleshy; oth-

The intriguing flowers are the main reason why gardeners are fascinated by *Ceropegia distincta* subspecies *haygarthii* and the other vines in this genus of tropical and subtropical plants.

ers are fibrous; and some are tuberous, the result of the different species evolving in areas with seasonal drought and terrains of varying soil qualities.

Ceropegias as a group are unusual houseplants. Except for the common *Ceropegia woodii* and its cousin tuberous types, the vines are too vigorous for casual indoor growing. Provided they get good light, warmth, and moving air, many will quickly fill a four-foot tomato-cage support and reach for more.

Flowers appear at the nodes, where both leaves and roots also form. They usually consist of a tube with hairs inside that point downward. The tube may be straight or have bends (*Ceropegia aristolochioides*) or bulges (*C. crassifolia, C. rupicola*). Its five corolla lobes (or petals) may be open (*C. stapeliiformis*) or joined at the tips (*C. ampliata*). The flowers are usually whitish, with combinations of bright green, brown, and maroon spots, stripes, and shading. The buds start out looking like small bullets, and as they grow they can develop bulges or curves, tops becoming umbrellas (*C. sandersonii, C. monteiroae*) or cages (*C. ampliata, C. armandii*). The bud of *C. devecchii* looks like a Buddhist *vajra* symbol before opening. *Ceropegia distincta* subspecies *haygarthii* resembles a spotted Venetian wineglass stuffed with little pillows and topped with a fuzzy antenna. The flowers can grow from almost nothing to 3½ inches long in little more than a week. Blooming is triggered by a combination of increasing day length and warmer nights. In late spring, when nighttime temperatures are rising and the daylight hours are lengthening, ceropegias such as *C. conrathii* respond with faster growth and start blooming. Others, such as *C. sandersonii,* wait until the heat of midsummer, and still others, such as *C. ampliata,* don't flower until the days begin to shorten noticeably in fall.

Growing Ceropegias

Soil quality does not seem to be very important for growing ceropegias successfully, but good drainage is vital. Regular applications of 20-20-20 fertilizer at half strength are beneficial during growth periods. The real key to a collection of gorgeously flowering ceropegias seems to be adequate warmth. They all benefit greatly from a warm summer spent outside in bright filtered light but out of direct sun. Most ceropegias are happy when temperatures are in the high 70s at all times, but they will tolerate cooler temperatures in winter while they are dormant. A sunny windowsill is all that some will require then.

Most of the ceropegias I have grown tend to slow down or go completely dormant in winter. Responding to their changed needs in winter is key to their well-being.

Ceropegia ampliata benefits from a summer spent in a sheltered spot outdoors. It grows best in a hanging basket, where it will flower profusely in late summer.

Many species develop seasonal roots that dry up and die off in the plant's dormant season. During winter, the tuberous types need to be kept dry (*C. conrathii* is especially prone to rot) and should be watered only when evidence of new growth appears in late spring. Many of the thinner vines (*C. woodii*, *C. ampliata*, *C. linearis*, *C. elegans*) can tolerate low light levels and will continue to grow slowly throughout the cooler months and can safely be watered. Thick, leafless vines like *C. devecchii* should be kept dry, but it's fine to water *C. stapeliiformis* if it is still growing. *C. crassifolia* develops fleshy roots to which it dies back completely, only to reemerge in late spring. (Don't throw out that empty-looking pot!)

PESTS AND DISEASES Ceropegias have relatively few pest problems. Tuberous types and some of the deciduous vines can harbor the occasional mealy bug. In the greenhouse or during the summer outside, a slug may find a tuber tasty. Plants are most vulnerable right after they move back inside after a summer spent outdoors. A ceropegia that has bloomed with an extraordinary number of flowers is especially susceptible to sudden death. The plant may have exhausted itself or its soil and be too weak to cope with the change in light and humidity that are part of moving inside. Other ceropegias may die suddenly from a fungal infection or rot. Once a thick stem has black spots on it, there is little you can do beyond cutting the growing tips off

Ceropegia denticulata **is easily propagated from cuttings. It flowers best when the vine is just a year or two old.**

the plant and trying to root them and discarding the rest.

Growing Ceropegias From Cuttings

The best way to a sustainable collection of abundantly flowering ceropegias is to take cuttings every year and discard the original plant after it's been in the same pot and soil for two years. (If you can't bear to discard the plant, at least repot it every two years.) Starting from scratch every two years is especially effective for vining types, which turn woody after a few years. Woody stems seem to lose vigor, but new stems sprout roots easily, and with new soil they will bloom more readily. Take cuttings any time the plant is growing. Allow the cut tip of a vine cutting to callus over for two to three days to prevent rotting. In spring or fall, put the cutting into either a clear plastic box or bag with a moistened mixture of half perlite and half peat moss until it develops roots. In summer, try curling the vines around in a pot or hanging basket on top of potting soil. In either case, keep the cuttings out of direct sunlight to prevent cooking them. If you successfully root cuttings, you'll have a number of plants that you can try growing in different areas of your home or garden. It's a useful way to find out where the plants thrive. Another advantage of multiples is that they serve as a form of insurance against losing the species from your collection. If you don't have luck or space for cuttings yourself, pass them on to friends who do. That way there's a chance that you can get a new start should you lose a rare plant.

Ceropegias to Grow at Home

Over the years I have grown many species from all parts of the *Ceropegia* world, except India and China, whose export policies make it extremely difficult to obtain living plant material or seeds. The following plants are among the easiest to grow and bring to flower. None of the vining plants are small. I grow vining types (*C. sandersonii, C. lugardae, C. distincta*) in seven- to ten-inch clay pots with a trellis made from an slightly modified tomato cage that forms a wire column on which the plants can easily climb. The tuberous types (*C. ampliata, C. leroyi*) are grown in hanging baskets of varying diameters. You can find more information about the plants discussed in this article and other *Ceropegia* species at http://SageReynolds.com.

Ceropegia ampliata

Native to South Africa, where it is found in Gauteng, Kwazulu-Natal, and the Cape provinces, this plant has fibrous roots and minuscule to invisible leaves. Unbelievable numbers of white and green flowers up to two inches long appear for about two weeks in September, completely covering the plant. *Ceropegia ampliata* is fairly easy to grow in ordinary well-draining potting soil. The plant trails and weakly attempts to climb before it begins to bloom and is best grown in a hanging basket. In summer, I hang the plant on the north side of my porch in bright light but away from direct sunlight and water it generously, like all my other plants in hanging baskets.

Ceropegia denticulata

This native of Tanzania is easy to keep and seems quite tame compared with some other varieties like *Ceropegia aristolochioides* and *C. elegans,* whose tendrils have to be controlled daily. Easily grown from cuttings, the plant has flower buds near almost every leaf in September. It thrives when grown outside for the summer, and the occasional cool night does not cause the demise of flower buds or other harm. During the early part of the summer, my plant was so small for so long that I set its pot and trellis into a pot where *C. ballyana* was growing (and not blooming). Now, several months later, they have entwined themselves so thoroughly, it will be difficult to separate the two. But it's easy to tell which vine is which: The leaves of *C. denticulata* are succulent and yellow-green with pointed ends; the leaves of *C. ballyana* are more succulent, slightly larger, and dark green with prominent central veins and round ends.

Ceropegia distincta subspecies haygarthii

Native to Angola and South Africa's Kwazulu-Natal and Cape provinces, it is one of the easiest ceropegias to grow. Only *Ceropegia woodii*, the common rosary vine, is easier. *C. distincta* subspecies *haygarthii* tolerates a wide range of conditions and will grow well in most home environments, though it may not bloom until it can be moved outside for the summer. This species is also less susceptible to rot if overwatered. The stems are a little more than ⅛-inch thick, the roots are fibrous, and the leaves are thin and deciduous. This vigorous plant will root where it touches the ground and easily fills a three-foot trellis. It's best to start new plants at least every two years if not every year, as the stems turn white after a year and seem less capable of supporting new growth. Flowers appear on new growth, and providing the growing area is warm enough, they will appear in profusion for a long period during the summer. With their fuzzy antennae, shaded corollas, and crisp maroon spots, they are delightfully comical. Temperature seems to be key, and I suspect that the species can be kept in continuous bloom in warmer climates, provided that the plants are repotted annually and fertilized heavily. I've had buds appear on my plants in early April as the days begin to lengthen noticeably, but all buds were aborted until nighttime temperatures stayed above 60°F.

Ceropegia monteiroae

This plant, another native of South Africa, is closely related to *C. sandersonii* and very similar in flower color and shape. It is fairly new in the marketplace, remarkably easy to grow, and a prolific bloomer. The bright chartreuse flowers are about three inches long and have a lively purple fringe on the lobes that moves in the slightest breeze.

Ceropegia sandersonii

Native to Mozambique and South Africa's Gauteng and Kwazulu-Natal provinces, this plant has very succulent, lance-shaped leaves, robust stems, and fleshy roots. It is fairly easy to grow and does best when it spends the summer outdoors in the same high shade that rhododendrons enjoy. Each spring, the plant sends up new growth from its roots. New stems give rise to a display of spectacular four-inch-long flowers. The vine may grow up to 12 feet long in the course of a summer outside. At the end of summer or sometime in fall, before you move the plant back into the house, cut it back drastically. Before winter I move the plant inside under the lights in my studio, cut it back, and water sparingly to prevent desiccation. The plant continues to grow more slowly through the winter.

Ceropegia stapeliiformis

Native to the Cape provinces of South Africa, *Ceropegia stapeliiformis* was one of the first ceropegias I collected and is one of the easiest to grow. In nature, the plant's stems grow horizontally along the ground toward a spot that offers dappled sunlight.

C. stapeliiformis thrives underneath shrubs, where greater moisture promotes root growth and leaf mold provides nutrients. Shrub branches also offer supports on which the plant can climb and display its flowers higher up, where they may be more easily found by pollinators.

For the collector, the plant's main attraction is its thick maroon- and gray-mottled snakelike stem, but its flowers are also surprisingly bizarre. When a new plant gets ready to bloom, its stem thins and starts to climb. Once the stem is about two feet above the

Ceropegia stapeliiformis blooms when the vine reaches about two feet in length, a bonus for anyone who grows it in a pot. Some tropical ceropegias won't bloom until the vines are longer than a typical garden or home greenhouse can accommodate.

roots, buds start to form, giving rise to numerous 2½-inch-long flowers. Their corollas open to expose a fuzzy white or pale green star. The plant seems to like a place in high shade where it gets some morning and afternoon sun. When I have grown it in full sun, the stem has always grown away from the light, snaking around pots to climb an *Abutilon* or *Pelargonium* before blooming. It has never set seeds, even though I have seen a lot of small flies on the corolla lobes while the flowers were open. To bring the plant into bloom in cultivation, it's best to take new cuttings each year. Simply break off new shoots that may already have formed roots and grow them in new soil.

Ceropegia stapeliiformis subspecies *serpentina* is a much shyer bloomer with a thinner, greenish stem that grows over three feet long before flowers form. One of my plants produced only one elegant flower—all green and white without any red in it—over the course of seven years. This year I put the pot on the ground in my garden. A stem rooted in the earth, sent a new shoot up a bamboo stake, and then produced four flowers at each node between July and October. (Maybe next year I'll take the rest of the shy bloomers and plant them in the garden soil instead of keeping them in pots.)

Stapeliads:
Sea Stars of the Desert

Gerald Barad

Stapeliads are a remarkable group of stem succulents with beautiful and intricate flower structures. The group is best known for two striking characteristics: the distinctive five-pronged flowers that look like sea stars and the incredible aroma that emanates from them. Stapeliad flowers vary in size from the immense 16-inch flowers of *Stapelia gigantea* to the tiny quarter-inch blooms of *Echidnopsis* species. Many of them have colorful hairs and sculptured surfaces, which are best seen through a hand lens. The perfume of stapeliad flowers is so captivating to flies that they will travel huge distances in order to be intoxicated by the scent. Unlike most other plants that use colors, scents, or nectar to lure insects to come and pollinate the flowers, stapeliads use pungent odors to attract insects that are attracted to rotting matter. Flies may even leave rotting carcasses to lay their eggs on stapeliad flowers. (Needless to say, the fly offspring never make it to adulthood.)

I became seriously interested in collecting and growing these plants about 50 years ago, when I was a young hospital intern. At that time my entire collection fit in a tiny greenhouse that covered an outside porch on our second-floor apartment. As the years passed, I eventually graduated to the 3,700-square-foot growing space that now houses my collection of more than 8,000 pots, many of which are stapeliads. I also grow a very varied group of cacti and succulents. My 50 years of desert wanderings

On the facing page is the striking one-inch flower of *Stapelia flavopurpurea,* enlarged to show detail. A hand lens comes in handy to appreciate the intricate structures of stapeliad flowers.

and greenhouse growing have been greatly enriched by these extraordinary plants, which have fascinated plant fanciers and botanists since the first specimens were introduced into Europe in the early 1600s.

In the wild, these plants grow in a wide range of habitats from the Canary Islands and southern Spain in the west, across North Africa to Israel in the east, south through the Arabian Peninsula to the Red Sea and on to the borders of the Arabian Sea. A number of species are native to India, and at least one of them is found in Myanmar (Burma). The vast majority of species are native to East Africa and South Africa where they grow in dry, rocky desert areas. Some of the larger hoodias are found growing on the open ground, but most of the species with more delicate stems are found under the cover of low-growing shrubs.

The celebrity of the stapeliad world, *Hoodia gordonii*, is a natural appetite suppressant. The plant is found in the Kalahari Desert of southern Africa, namely Botswana, Namibia, Angola, and South Africa. The local San people have known about the appetite-suppressing abilities of this plant for countless generations and have used the plant when food was scarce during long marches and hunting trips. *Hoodia gordonii* is now being cultivated in large quantities, and dried material from the plant is widely sold in natural food stores.

A few stapeliad species are used as food plants. The stems of *Caralluma edulis*, from

Difficult to grow in cultivation, *Pseudolithos caput-viperae* and other members in this small genus of stapeliads found only in parts of Somalia have an intriguing rocklike appearance and unearthly looking flowers.

Stapeliad flowers give off pungent odors rather than sweet scents to lure pollinators attracted by the perfume of rotting matter. The scheme pays off for this *Pseudolithos migiurtinus,* which has captured the attention of a fly.

India and other areas bordering the Indian Ocean and the Red Sea, are eaten, and the plant is thought to be helpful in treating diabetes by some traditional healers. On expedition in Somalia I encountered nomadic herdsmen who eat some of the rarest stapeliads, *Whitesloanea crassa* and several of the *Pseudolithos* species, as a moisture-rich snack. Locally it is referred to as *dinah,* which means little turtle.

Stapeliad Pollination

Stapeliads have a unique and astonishingly elaborate pollination mechanism. Most higher plants produce granular pollen on the anthers of their stamens, the male parts of the flower. To achieve fertilization, these pollen grains are transferred to the receptive surface of the stigma by a variety of vectors, such as pollinating insects, birds, and bats. The stapeliads are different. Their pollen is produced in the form of a solid mass of pollen cells called a pollinium. The only other group of plants that have similar structures, and are pollinated in this manner, are the orchids. The foul odors and red or brown colors of the flowers of many stapeliad species attract carrion flies and gnats, the plants' principal pollinators. When they visit the flowers, they sip nectar and frequently lay their eggs, as they would when they visit dead animals or animal droppings. As they move about the flower, a specialized structure, the corpusculum, attaches to a bristle on the proboscis or leg of the insect. As the insect struggles to free itself, the entire pollinating apparatus (the pollinarium) is pulled away from the flower. Two separate pollen sacs or pollinia are attached to the pollinarium and are carried with the insect as it visits the next flower. On the inner edge of each pollinium is a microscopic rod-shaped structure that I have named the pollinium key. The receptive area of the flower is a groove, the staminal lock, which is open toward the base of the flower and narrows toward the top. (Full details of this process as well as descriptive diagrams and macrophotographs can be found on my website: http://www.cactus-mall.com/stapeliad/pollin.html. The site also includes detailed information about the process of artificial pollination I've developed over the years.)

Growing Stapeliads

Stapeliads are not easy to cultivate in pots. Over the years I've had many exciting successes as well as a greater number of failures. These plants do quite well in the warmer parts of the year but are frequently lost to root rot during the winter months. Growing methods vary greatly in the different parts of the world where these plants are cultivated. A method that may be successful in a warm, humid climate may not work in a dry, desert environment. In the frost-free areas of the American South, many of the stapelias can be grown in well-drained garden beds. In Hawaii, *Stapelia gigantea* has naturalized, and in some areas it is considered an invasive weed, particularly in dry forests and open areas. The cultural methods described here have been successful in the temperate areas of North America where the plants must be grown indoors in the home or in a greenhouse.

GROWING MEDIA Stapeliad roots require excellent aeration. They need well-drained soil that doesn't hold too much water. I use my own mix, made up of equal parts inorganic particles and coarse organic matter. I blend two parts pumice (sold widely as Dry Stall and found in farm stores catering to horse owners) with one part Turface MVP (high-fired clay particles) and three parts Scotts Metro-Mix 360 coir formula (which contains a high proportion of coconut fiber, or coir). Growers who cultivate just a few plants can make a satisfactory mix by blending equal parts perlite and African violet growing medium, both available in most garden centers. The perlite is a bit unsightly as it percolates to the soil surface, but it can easily be hidden with a mulch layer of coarse gravel or small stones. None of these mixes provide adequate nutrients and must be supplemented with liquid fertilizers such as Dyna-Gro. When the plants are in active growth during the warm months of the year, I use liquid fertilizer at the manufacturer's recommended concentration with every watering.

TEMPERATURES Stapeliads come from warm regions and do best when night temperatures are above 60°F. In order to economize on fuel, I keep some areas of my greenhouse at about 50ºF. Most stapeliads have been able to tolerate this temperature, but a few choice species, such as those in the genus *Edithcolea,* don't tolerate it and should not be exposed to temperatures below 60ºF. On sunny winter days the temperature in my greenhouse rises into the 70s and 80s. As spring advances, these higher temperatures occur more often, giving rise to new growth and the formation of flower buds. Plants that are grown in heated apartments can be kept growing year-round as long as they are given adequate light. Many growers have been successful growing stapeliads under fluorescent lights and bringing them to bloom. I raise stapeliads from seed by growing them under a metal halide lamp in winter; by springtime the seedlings are strong enough to transplant.

LIGHT In the wild, stapeliads grow in places where light intensities can be very high, and most protect themselves by growing under shrub cover. In my New Jersey greenhouse the plants tolerate full sun very well, since the brightest light here is much less

The biggest challenge facing anyone interested in growing *Stapelia scitula* and its fabulous relatives is their sensitivity to rot during the colder months.

Huernianthus 'Alexis' was produced by the author by crossing *Huernia longituba* and *Stapelianthus kerandrenae* during experiments with hybridization, one of his specialties.

intense than that of desert areas; the coverings on my greenhouse further reduce the light intensity. If you grow stapeliads as houseplants, give them the brightest exposure available.

WATERING Water stapeliads only when the soil has become dry, and then just enough to moisten the soil. Soggy feet will quickly kill these plants. How fast the soil dries out depends on the temperature of the air, the amount of sunshine the plant receives, and the porosity of its pot. Clay pots lose water much faster than plastic ones. During very warm spells in summer, they may need daily watering. During cool, overcast conditions, they may not need water for several weeks.

As desert dwellers, stapeliads don't seem to have evolved any resistance to the fungi that can attack them under cool and wet conditions. To help prevent losing my plants to rot, I used to water them very little during the winter months. However, I lost a number of small plants because they dried out too much. Small pots should be watched very carefully—they may need water more often. A good way to determine whether a plant needs watering is to pull the plastic label out of the pot and check its surface. If it is coated with dark, moist particles the plant should not be watered. If the label is dry and shows only a slight coating of dust, it's time to water.

PESTS AND PESTICIDES Mealy bugs are the major pest of stapeliads. They appear as white, waxy masses on the stems or roots of the plants. Treat mealy bugs by removing the masses with a cotton swab soaked in rubbing alcohol.

Root mealy bugs need to be controlled with a soil drench. If you are treating only a few plants at a time, shake the soil off the roots and rinse the plants with a forceful spray of water. Then dip the root ball in horticultural oil solution (one tablespoon of horticultural oil to one quart of water) or a solution containing potassium salts, such as Safer insecticidal soap. After the roots have dried, repot the plants in fresh soil.

Propagating Stapeliads

Propagation is a fun way to learn more about stapeliads. Though artificial pollination is a fabulous way to get to know the plants up close, it is by no means the only way to propagate them at home. It's much easier to buy seeds, take cuttings, or make a graft.

SEED PROPAGATION Stapeliads are easily raised from seeds. Pure species seeds are difficult to obtain. Since many plants are pollinated by flies, hybridization is quite common. If you merely want to observe the seedlings develop, you can use fly-pollinated seeds. A reliable source for seeds of known parentage is the International Asclepiad Society. Their seeds, described in an annual seed list, are collected from wild plants or from controlled pollination of plants in cultivation. (Contact them at http://www.cactus-mall.com/ias/index.html#membership.) More ambitious growers may want to attempt artificial pollination.

Fresh seeds usually germinate within a few days after planting. I prefer to start seeds in my home under high-pressure sodium light in mid-November. It's also fine to start a small number of seeds under fluorescent light, provided they are kept close to the tube. Seedlings started in this manner will be ready for transplanting into separate pots in spring, and some will flower the following summer. I use a soil mix similar to the one I use for adult plants, but I screen out large particles. Stapeliad seeds have a narrow end at which the root emerges. Use a pencil to make a small hole in the soil and plant the seeds with the narrow end down. Keep the soil moist and warm during germination. When the seedlings emerge, less moisture is needed, but continue to water daily because they dry out fast under the sodium light.

CUTTINGS The most common propagation method is via cuttings. Many stapeliads have jointed stems that can be separated and potted after a few hours of drying (to avoid rotting, freshly cut surfaces must be allowed to callus over before planting). In warm soil, the cuttings will root in a week or two.

GRAFTING Some species are particularly difficult to keep alive on their own roots. In these cases, grafting may be the best option. This is done by joining the top of one plant (the scion) to the understock of another, more vigorous species. Many sturdy stapeliad species have been used as understocks. I have found the tubers of *Ceropegia woodii* 'String of Hearts' to be very reliable rootstocks. I have also used *Stapelia gigantea* with good results. Grafting should be done in warm weather, when both the stock and the scion are in active growth. Use a very sharp knife or a razor blade to make a clean, flat cut on the stock plant and a similar one on the scion. Clean the knife with alcohol before making each cut to avoid introducing fungus spores to the cut surfaces. In most cases a little pressure between the two parts will force out air bubbles and excess fluid. Rubber bands suspended from the top of the scion to the bottom of the pot can be used to hold the two parts in place; in about 24 hours they will hold together without the rubber band. If the scion is an elongated stem like that often found in stapelias, I make a brace out of wire to support it and then use rubber bands on the brace. Successful grafts will usually start to show new growth in two to four weeks.

Stapeliads for Beginners

Stapeliads are not the easiest plants to cultivate in the home because they are very sensitive to rot. Below are plants from three genera that are among the least difficult to grow. Be sure to observe the plants carefully and follow the care tips in this chapter.

Huernia

A large number of huernias are available from specialty dealers, and they make good houseplants. Most of the species are mat-forming or creeping. The flowers are moderate in size and rarely exceed two inches in diameter. Many species have flowers decorated with hairs and small bumps (papillae). These remarkable succulents may present a challenge to the new grower, but bringing them into bloom is ample reward for the effort.

Orbea variegata

This plant, known as *Stapelia variegata* for many years, is probably the most variable of all stapeliads. The size of the flower may vary anywhere from two to three inches in diameter, and many color forms are known. Most can be recognized by their mottled yellow and brown colors and the distinctive ring, or annulus. Many forms are native to Table Mountain in Western Cape Province, South Africa, where they flourish in the frequent mists that settle on the rocky slopes. They are reliable pot plants and will grow and flower in a bright window. As with all other stapeliads, they require a porous soil and should not be overwatered.

Stapelia gigantea

This species grows quite well as a houseplant if it is given the conditions described above. It has some of the largest flowers in the entire group—some plants produce flowers 12 to 15 inches across. If it is grown in a small living room, it may have to be removed when it flowers, since the scent is very strong and quite foul.

Considered some of the easier stapeliads to grow and fairly simple to obtain, huernias like *Huernia occulta* may be a good entry to this challenging plant group.

Growing Cacti and Other Succulents on Windowsills and Under Lights

Stephen Maciejewski

Cacti and succulents were not my first love. My obsession with the green world actually started with passionflowers, gravitated to orchids, then moved on to gesneriads and various tropicals. I longed for lush, exuberant growth; with this rather narrow view of the plant world, I had trouble appreciating something like a living stone (*Lithops*). To my eyes, succulents and cacti looked unfriendly, and many of them just seemed to look alike. Eventually, though, a second, more careful look revealed nearly endless variations among these fascinating plants, and I now see their adaptations as a living testament to evolution. Today these tough little guys are my constant companions, arranged on multishelf light carts and divided among the 18 windows of my three-story row house.

It's easy to grow beautiful, award-winning succulents and cacti without the benefit of a greenhouse, whether you live in a small apartment with a view to the north or, like me, in a row house bathed in light.

When starting a collection, the most important thing is to know which kinds of growing conditions you can provide; then acquire plants that thrive in those environments. Some basic criteria for deciding whether plants go on the windowsill or

Observe how the sunlight travels across your windows throughout the day and the seasons, and place plants according to their light requirements. Be sure to turn them periodically to avoid uneven growth.

on a light cart include size, height, shape, light and temperature preferences, and dormancy needs. Cacti and other succulents are wildly various in their requirements; you'll need to do some research to find out what each plant requires and then try to approximate the conditions it needs to thrive. Don't be afraid to ask questions about growing media, pots, watering and fertilizer requirements, humidity and air-circulation needs, and disease and insect problems. Don't expect to turn into a succulent expert overnight, and don't be discouraged if not every plant you acquire survives. Take it one step at a time, and as you learn how to make these plants happy, all those empty windowsills, neglected closets, and dark basements can now become productive growing areas.

If the idea of growing plants described as "living rocks," "flowering stones," or "pieces of architecture" is appealing, or if you have a lust for almost endless variations on a theme, then it's time to extend your art collection to include the world of cacti and succulents. This can also be good for your social life—since I joined the Philadelphia Cactus and Succulent Society and have exhibited at the Philadelphia Flower Show, I've met a lot of people who share my passion and obsession for plants.

Growing Cacti and Succulents on Windowsills

Knowing in what directions the windows face is critical when setting up a healthy indoor growing space that's completely reliant on natural light. For sun-loving succulents, southern exposure is usually best, but in summer a southern window may require a sheer curtain to protect the plants from burning during the hottest part of the day. Eastern exposure is second best, followed by western and northern exposures. And then there are the in-betweens like northeastern and southwestern exposures, which may be just perfect for some plants.

Exposure isn't all you have to think about when it comes to light, however. Light intensity depends very much on the placement of the window. Upper-floor windows usually get more light than those on lower floors, which is especially critical in winter, when the sun sits lower in the sky. On the upside, if you have deciduous trees near your windows, you may actually get more light coming in everywhere in winter when the branches are bare. Then there is the weather to contend with. Bleak skies for weeks on end make it hard for plants to flourish, and if the plants get too close to the cold glass during the winter months they may suffer cold damage. No matter what the season or the floor, aim to keep your windows clean to take advantage of all available light.

Some cacti and succulents require more intense light than what they can get naturally through the windows and will thrive only if they can spend at least part of the day under artificial lights.

If your windowsills get crowded over time and you are adding glass or wire shelves or windowsill extenders to increase your space, bear in mind that the farther the plants are from the window, the less intense the light will be. Finally, unless you want lopsided growth, give each plant a quarter turn every few weeks. As you assess your windowsill growing spaces, take note of the many microclimates they offer. This is an invitation to experiment to find out exactly where individual plants do best—and where they fare poorly—in your home.

I've noticed that taller plants and ones that need lots of winter light do better in windows on higher floors because of the angle of the winter sun. I've found that a drafty windowsill is a perfect spot to place a cactus that needs a cool winter rest in order to flower. I have also learned through sad experience to keep an eye on any plant that gets pushed into the corner of a crowed shelf. Too often this pocket of dead air space becomes the ideal location for insects to flourish.

Growing Cacti and Succulents Under Artificial Lights

There are lots of advantages to using artificial lights, not least that you can provide your succulents with an endless summer even if the weather outside is atrocious for weeks on end. The most important point to keep in mind is that it's light you want to impart to your plants, not heat. Incandescent bulbs, the most common lights used to illuminate homes, do provide light but also generate much more heat than fluorescents; they can burn your plants.

LIGHTING OPTIONS

The most economical lights for cultivating succulents are cool and warm white fluorescent light tubes, which produce a lot of light but little heat. For best results, most growers keep their plants under four fluorescent tubes and use a combination of both warm and cool fluorescent bulbs. Available at large hardware stores, the tubes come in two-, four-, and eight-foot lengths, with the four-foot-ones probably the handiest size for most homes. Eight-foot fixtures and tubes may be tempting, especially if you consider that the light intensity is greatest around the center of the tubes, but they are harder to maneuver, not always available, and more costly than shorter ones. No matter which length of tubes you choose, replace all grow lights once a year.

There are also a number of special, and more costly, plant-lighting systems to choose from and even specialty lighting stores that cater to the needs of indoor plant growers. High-intensity discharge (HID) lights (both metal halide and high-pressure sodium) are the most powerful. Low-pressure sodium lamps are also available.

A light cart greatly increases the available growing space. To avoid heat damage, keep plants at a safe distance from the lights.

Crassula 'Morgan's Pink' makes an impressive clump within a few years. Its bright-colored late-winter blooms and unfussy nature make it a good windowsill plant.

HOMEMADE LIGHT CARTS

It's quite easy to construct a light cart for use with fluorescents. Assuming that you opt for four-foot tubes, start with a two-by-four-foot piece of plywood. Attach a two-by-two-inch surround. Cover the whole with two layers of plastic sheeting. Then lay a two-by-four-foot section of plastic egg-crate grid (used in lighting fixtures) on top of the plastic-wrapped plywood. (The egg-crate grid provides a sturdy platform on which to position your plants and makes it possible to water them freely without moving them. Excess water simply drips through the crate and collects on the plastic sheeting, keeping your pots from standing in water and avoiding rot.) Install two shop lights with two tubes each for each shelf (or four tubes per shelf). Then build a simple frame for the shelves. For a three-tier light cart, use four 2-by-4s, six feet in length, for the uprights and six additional 2-by-4s for supports for the shelves. Attach heavy-duty casters to the bottom of the frame to make your light cart mobile. You can attach the light fixture to the bottom of the shelf above either by screwing it into the plywood or by using plastic ties attached to hooks in the plywood.

Finally, purchase a heavy-duty appliance timer so you don't need to run home every evening to turn the lights off. Plug your lights into the timer and plug the timer into an electrical socket. For added safety, use a surge protector. Keep the lights on for about 15 hours per day in the winter months. Increase the length of time by two hours during the summer if you keep your plants inside year-round. (If you're planning to add lots of light units and gadgets and have doubts about your wiring, consult an electrician before you get to work.)

STORE-BOUGHT LIGHT CARTS

I have also acquired a number of multishelf, ready-made metal light carts with lights attached to adjustable chains. These are more versatile than homemade carts with fixed shelves, since you can lower the lights to just above the plants. This is useful for

certain plants that grow best when they are nearly touching the light, including *Ariocarpus fissuratus, Aeonium arboreum* 'Atropurpureum' crest, *Avonia alstonii,* and *Ceraria namaquensis.*

I also collect wide-mouth plastic jar lids about an inch high and use them along with inverted pots to elevate some plants closer to the tubes. Place plants that need the most intense light toward the

Euphorbia millotii thrives under artificial lights, but it doesn't tolerate strong summer sun in a western or southern window.

Available in different sizes and colors, rock mulches echo the surface colors and textures found in the native habitats of many cacti and succulents. *Echeveria elegans*, above, models four common types.

center of the tubes, where the light is strongest. Move those requiring less light toward the ends or around the perimeter. To boost the intensity of the fluorescents, paint the walls or surrounds matte white. (Various devices like mirrors, aluminum foil, and reflective mylar are often recommended to increase light levels around the plants, but in my view white paint works best.) A three- or four-tiered light cart gives off a lot of light. Take advantage of the intensity: Position some larger plants around the cart on the floor or elevate them next to the shelves.

Also consider the heat generated by the fixtures when placing plants. The bottom shelf is always a little cooler than upper shelves because it isn't warmed from below by the light tubes.

If you think growing cacti and other succulents on a cart under lights is too limiting, you're in for a surprise. If you use a two-by-four-foot shelf and choose small plants, you'll likely be able to satisfy your collecting urges. That space can hold up to 288 square pots measuring 2 inches in diameter, 171 square pots measuring 2½ inches, 128 square pots measuring 3 inches, or 72 square pots measuring 4 inches. Of course, you'll want to leave space between the plants when they grow over the sides of the pots. There are many cacti and succulents that will fit into even the smallest pot at maturity, such as the plant shown below.

Growing Media

The most important quality of a soil mix for cacti and succulents is good drainage. I usually use a blend originally developed by Gerald Barad (whose article on stapeliads starts on page 52). It's an open, porous mix that drains quickly and is made up of three parts Metro-Mix 560, two parts Perma-Till, and one part Turface. (Metro-Mix 560 is made up of 20 to 30 percent sphagnum moss, 5 to 15 percent horticultural perlite, 5 to 15 percent processed bark ash, 35 to 45 percent composted pine bark,

This five-year-old *Adromischus mariannae* var. *herrei* is only a couple of inches tall. It needs bright light and water from October to April and a spot away from the center of the light cart during summer dormancy.

Bright light brings out the pink on the leaf margins of ×*Graptoveria* **'Silver Star' crest. Sensitive to overwatering, the plant is more active in winter than in summer but never goes completely dormant.**

and 20 to 30 percent processed coconut coir. Perma-Till is the trade name for stalite, an expanded slate material. It looks like pea gravel, but each particle is filled with tiny air spaces. Turface is a clay product often used on athletic fields. It prevents soil compaction, improves moisture absorption, and helps the mix to stay porous.) Keep in mind that even among cacti and other succulents, drainage and nutrient needs vary. You may want to customize the texture and composition of the mix for plants with special needs. But whichever blend you use, try to be consistent for plants with similar requirements to ensure that all pots dry out at about the same rate. Your goal is to streamline your operation so that the ongoing maintenance doesn't consume too much of your time and keep you from enjoying your hobby.

Pots and Labels

You'll need to decide whether plastic or clay pots suit you. Both have pluses and minuses. Plastic pots are lighter, cheaper, and hold more moisture. Clay provides better air circulation and aids in evaporation and cooling. The extra weight of clay also adds stability and prevents your plants from toppling over. It's a good idea to label every plant. List the botanical name along with the common name, the date you potted the plant, and other information, including where you obtained the plant and specific growing conditions, such as dormancy requirements (and leave

To help you fine-tune plant care and avoid confusion, label all pots with the plants' botanical names and the dates that they moved into your home or were started from seeds or cuttings.

room to record the awards the plant may receive). For more reasons to label your plants, see the article on conservation, page 8. Over the years I've found that a No. 2 pencil is the most durable marker for pot labels. As your collection grows, it also helps to keep a written record of your plants, keyed to a code marked on the pot, especially for those all-too-common occasions when the label has disappeared or faded.

Watering and Fertilizer Applications

There is no single answer as to how often you should water your plants. There are just too many variables—the growing mix, pot type and size, temperature, humidity, and each plant's changing needs throughout the year. If you stick with one kind of pot, you'll learn to judge just how dry the plant is when you pick it up. You may also want to try a little experiment that can be very helpful in gauging how all the factors listed above influence how quickly your pots dry out: Take four pots of equal size, shape, and material. Fill all of them with the same mix. Water the pots and place them in the same location. After three days, spill the contents of one pot and check the moisture content. Do the same with the rest of the pots after five, seven, and nine days. This test should give you some guidance as to how often you should water plants in your home.

Remember, though, that each individual plant's growth cycle determines its watering schedule. Some succulents go through a five-month dormant period that may last from November to March. There may be obvious signs like leaf drop, but in some cases you just have to know the plant to determine what it needs at any given time. Watering when a plant is dormant may cause it to rot. But in a heated house, especially under artificial lights, you may need to give a dormant plant some water occasionally, maybe mist it now and then, and then return to more frequent watering when you start to see new growth.

For succulents that don't go through dormancy, proper watering may mean once or twice a week or bimonthly or even less frequently. If in doubt, it's usually better to wait a little longer. Some succulents rot very easily. If you're not sure whether it's time to water, there's a way to check, and the technique is similar to checking on a bird in the oven. Simply stick a label into the soil: If it comes out clean, without any soil particles attached to it, better get out the watering can. In any case, never leave pots in standing water, as this will invariably lead to root rot. When you develop a watering schedule, you'll find that it's also a good idea to water on the same day(s) every week. And if you're anything like me, you'll need to mark the schedule on your calendar. This way you won't waste time wondering when you last watered your plants.

I also use various fertilizers and Superthrive (a vitamin and hormone booster) on my plants. I usually use soluble powder or liquid fertilizers and not the pellet forms, since they may continue to stimulate growth beyond the normal growing period. Generally I use a balanced fertilizer like 20-20-20 and apply it according to the instructions on the package and only during the growing season.

You can also spend lots of time searching for the perfect watering tool. The number of plants in your collection, their location, and even your physical strength will influence your decision. If you favor watering cans, ones with long spouts are very useful. A 50-foot accordion hose attached to the kitchen faucet has worked well for me. With the hose and an extension wand, I can freely roam around the house and not be burdened by the weight of a dripping watering can.

Temperatures and Air Circulation

Obviously, you'll set the house thermostat to the setting that suits you; your cacti and succulents will adjust. But be careful during the winter months: Make sure that your plants don't touch cold window glass, broil over a radiator, or dry out near an air vent.

At the same time, be aware that some plants prefer a cool winter rest and that some need cool winter temperatures to flower. You'll need to find a microclimate somewhere in the house for each plant with special winter requirements, perhaps on a porch or by a drafty window. In general, though, the relatively dry air in most homes will be fine for succulents, especially if you provide ventilation. I use an oscillating fan year-round for all plants, whether they grow on a windowsill or on a light cart. Good air circulation helps keep the plants dry, dislodges debris, makes the environment less inviting for pests, helps prevent diseases, and lessens temperature extremes.

Keeping Plants Healthy

To keep your plants insect- and disease-free, practice good sanitation by removing all plant debris from around the plants and pots and keeping your growing area clean. Dried leaves and other dead plant material make cozy spots for insects to hide and breed. I have often found that plants tucked away in corners, in hard-to-reach, somewhat neglected spots, are usually the ones that attract insects. Prevention is essential and saves you lots of time in the long run.

When an insect problem does develop, choose the least toxic control option available to keep yourself and others safe. A spray of horticultural oil (which smothers insects) is one of the most effective and least toxic pest controls that you can use. Using a quart spray bottle filled with water, add one tablespoon of horticultural oil, neem oil, or any light cooking oil, and three drops of dish-washing detergent. Shake the bottle repeatedly and spray the entire plant with the emulsion.

For mealy bugs, which look like bits of cotton stuck on a plant, spraying with 70 percent isopropyl (rubbing) alcohol is very effective. Let the plant dry before you return it to bright sunlight to avoid sunburn. Repeat the alcohol spraying every week for three weeks in a row to ensure that any emerging insects are killed.

To tackle scale, coat the plant with an oil spray and then use a small soft brush like a toothbrush to gently remove the scale from the affected stem or leaf.

Summering Cacti and Other Succulents Outdoors

I put many of my plants outside in the garden in spring and keep them there over the summer, moving them back into the house in early fall. The time outdoors makes up for any limitations the plants endured indoors.

When you first put your plants out, avoid sunburn by setting them out of direct sunlight. Place them under a tree or in another shady spot, then let them gradually

Mammillaria elongata usually forms a cluster of finger-size plants. Due to mutation, this specimen is crested, producing attractively wavelike growth. Though *Mammillaria elongata* tolerates it well if its growing medium dries out completely, many other succulents need close monitoring to maintain a balance between overwatering and extreme drought.

adjust to the new light levels. Never underestimate summer rains. A few days of heavy downpours can rot your prized succulents. You may need to cover your plants or move them inside to avoid a deadly soaking. If possible, ask someone to keep an eye on your plants when you go away on an extended vacation.

When it's time to move your plants back into the house during the fall, carefully check for insects. I spray all of my cacti and other succulents with horticultural oil to avoid inadvertently importing pests into the house.

Starter Cacti and Succulents for Growing Indoors

Start with the easy ones! A well-grown common plant looks much better than a sickly rare one. And in any case, a plant that is difficult for one grower could turn out to be easy for you. Size and shape do matter when it comes to the number of plants crowded on a narrow windowsill. Try to start with plants that are manage-able and stay that way, but don't be afraid to experiment with ones that can mature, under ideal conditions, into large, treelike structures. Although some plants do get to be colossal, it could take decades growing there in your house. And don't forget that prickly plants should be kept where they cannot harm unwary people or curious pets.

Easy Cacti for the Windowsill

Epiphyllum Species and Cultivars

Often called orchid cacti, members of the genus *Epiphyllum* come in a variety of leaf and flower shapes. The exotic-looking flowers exhibit a rich and gorgeous palette of colors, are often fragrant, produce colorful fruits, and display a flamboy-ant design. Some can be grown upright, while others grow best in hanging bas-kets. They can also become quite large. They grow best in indirect light and should have cooler night temperatures, especially in the winter, to encourage flowering. The potting mix should remain moist and not be allowed to dry out.

Epiphyllum oxypetalum is an epiphytic cactus that grows in the tropics on trees and cliffs. Better known as queen of the night or night-blooming cereus, this cac-tus has strong branches with long, leathery green leaves and lots of ropelike aerial roots. It likes rich soil with good drainage. In winter, it requires little water and is very forgiving. Should you forget about it and let it dry out, it will still spring back after a drink. The plant can grow up to over six feet, which makes it a good candi-date to summer outside, under a tree or in another spot that's out of direct sun. When it blooms, it's time to throw a party. At dusk, the buds quickly unfurl. Keep your eyes glued to the plant and you can actually see them open. The creamy flow-ers are spectacular and rather peculiar, in that they grow out of the notches on the leaflike stems. It is a miraculous sight and, to top it off, the flowers are also won-derfully fragrant. The only drawback is that by the following morning, the flowers are completely spent and limp. This is a great plant to share with friends. Just cut off a section, stick it in a pot, and soon you'll have another plant.

Myrtillocactus geometrizans

This handsome blue-green treelike cactus, commonly called blue flame, can grow to 13 feet tall in the wild, but it is quite manageable for years on a windowsill. The crested form has been nicknamed dinosaur cactus because of its ridged and con-torted growth. Place the plant in a warm spot where it gets lots of sunlight, and summer it outdoors. Be careful with watering. Give it just enough so it doesn't wither away.

Easy Succulents for the Windowsill

Beaucarnea recurvata

Mine sits by a south-facing window in a 14-inch terra-cotta pot perched on an inverted pot. I share this choice plant with my Siamese cat, Feathers, who loves to swat and chew on the long straplike leaves. My pony-tail palm, with its ten-inch caudex, or swollen base, once was a show plant, but all those feline tooth marks have put an end to its ribbon days.

Dioscorea

Many plants in this genus grow well on a windowsill. An individual may go dormant during the cold months, but even if it drops its leaves, the caudex is still attractive and generates lots of questions from curious visitors. *Dioscorea mexicana* (syn. *macrostachya*), sometimes called the turtleback plant, develops a huge caudex. Its heavily veined, heart-shaped shiny leaves taper to a point. The vine often needs the support of a wire hoop or trellis to climb on. This plant really does provide year-round pleasure. Summer it outside and move it back indoors for the winter.

Hoya Wax Vines

There are numerous species and varieties to choose from for an interesting variety of leaf shapes, flower colors, and fragrances. All are fairly tough and easy-to-grow plants, most often trained on wire hoops. Purchase a hoop or make your own out of a tomato cage. (Cut the upright wires, and then bend them to follow the circle. Near the base, bend the wire out so that you use it to anchor the hoop in the pot.)

Then wrap the vine around the hoop. Eventually you'll form a lovely living wreath of leaves. Some of my ribbon-winning hoyas include *Hoya australis, Hoya carnosa* 'Rubra', *Hoya cinnamomifolia*, and *Hoya obovata*.

Jatropha podagrica

This plant looks like a genie's bottle, hence its common name bottleplant. It may drop its three-lobed, dark green leaves in fall but always puts on a display of its red blooms in early March. At times, it will flower even without leaves. The naked plant then looks like a handsome tan bottle holding a bouquet of small red flowers.

The swollen stem, or caudex, is the main attraction of *Dioscorea mexicana* once it drops its leaves in fall.

Easy Cacti to Grow Under Lights

Leuchtenbergia principis

This cactus forms a rosette of long, blue-green tubercles with purplish blotches at their tips, each growing to about five inches. Each tubercle is tipped with an areole from which four-inch-long, paper-thin, straw-colored spines emerge, giving this native of the Chihuahuan Desert a somewhat disheveled look. It grows to about 14 inches high in its native habitat and takes about six years to mature and produce yellow flowers, which emerge from its center. Summer it outdoors and move it inside during its winter dormancy. To prevent rot in winter, water the tuberous-rooted plant only to keep it from drying out completely.

Mammillaria karwinskiana f. nejapesis

Growing solitary or in clumps, individual plants of this furry *Mammillaria* can measure up to four inches in height and diameter. Large white spines show off nicely against the color of the plant body. The wool on my specimen gives the appearance of a close-cropped neat haircut, but there is great variability, and others may be nearly bald or have hair sticking out here and there, more like a punk haircut. Summer this cactus outside and try keeping it in a cool spot in winter; water only to prevent it from drying out completely.

Melocactus matanzanus

This eye-catching cactus is sometimes called dwarf Turk's cap after the reddish-brown caplike structure, the cephalium, on top of the mature plant, which is pale green and measures about 3½ inches in diameter. The cephalium gives rise to pink flowers and lilac-pink fruits. The genus *Melocactus* is native to the Americas and the West Indies; *Melocactus matanzanus* is native to Cuba. For a photo, see page 98.

Pereskia aculeata f. godseffiana

The plants in this very unusual and primitive cactus genus look like shrubby vines and are not considered succulent. Easily pruned, this *Pereskia* makes a good houseplant with waxy, shimmering leaves that are pink or bronze-green mother-of-pearl on the surface and purplish red on the undersides. Summer it outdoors and move it inside in fall, giving it less water but never letting it dry out completely.

More Easy Cacti to Grow Under Lights

Easy Succulents to Grow Under Lights

Dorstenia foetida

The flower of *Dorstenia foetida* looks like a fig turned inside out. Called the hypanthodium, the strange, otherworldly pale green inflorescence is flat with tentacle-like protuberances. The plant grows to about eight inches tall and has many short, thick branches. Native to Yemen, the species loves heat but doesn't need intense sunlight: a perfect plant for the light cart. When it's in growth, water freely, but keep it dry when it's leafless.

Pachypodium brevicaule

This squat plant with a smooth-textured, silvery caudex may grow a foot high and reach a diameter of three feet. If the plant loses its leaves, cut back on watering. Summer it outdoors.

Lots of light, warmth, even watering, and good drainage are essential to prevent *Pachypodium brevicaule* from rotting.

Pelargonium rapaceum

This delicate-looking tuberous plant has long and narrow, feathery leaves that are soft and hairy. At maturity the plant can reach a diameter of four inches. Native to the Cape provinces of South Africa, it has a definite dormant period starting around May. Mine grows during fall and winter in a small clay pot with a well-drained mix and flourishes on a light cart perched on an inverted pot, almost touching the lights.

More Easy Succulents to Grow Under Lights

Aeonium arboreum 'Atropurpureum'

Albuca spiralis

Aloe krapohliana var. *dumoulinii*

Aloe suprafoliata

Aloe 'Black Beauty'

Aloe 'Quick Silver'

Brighamia insignis

Ceraria namaquensis

Crassula exilis

Deuterocohnia brevifolia

Echeveria minima

Echeveria pulvinata

Euphorbia flanaganii f. *cristata*

Ficus palmeri

Gasteria glomerata

Haworthia cooperi f. *venusta*

Pelargonium cotyledonis

Plectranthus ernstii

Propagating Cacti and Succulents

Susan Aument

If you have been growing succulents for any length of time, you probably already know a little bit about propagating them. You may have seen the tiny aerial roots emerging on the stem of a sedum or echeveria and removed a piece with roots attached and planted it in the ground. Voilà! New plant. You may have noticed that propagating succulents is a very simple and fun way by which to expand your collection and make it more diverse for very little money or effort.

But you may not know that many of the plants on your windowsill may be rare or endangered in their native habitats. What has kept these plants alive in cultivation over the years is propagation by succulent lovers, including collectors, nursery people, scientists, and home gardeners. So sow some seed, take some cuttings, reap the rewards, and share them with your friends.

Starting From Seed

Growing plants from seed is a good way to acquire some of the rarer forms of cacti and other succulents that you may not be able to find in your local garden center. It's also a good way to acquire a lot of plants for very little money, especially useful if you'd like to incorporate a large number of plants into a display or an outdoor landscape.

Enlarged to show detail, the split-open fruit of *Mammillaria prolifera* reveals its seeds, ready to plant. Propagating rare or endangered species from seed is a good way to keep the plants alive in cultivation.

Seed catalogs that specialize in succulents offer a huge array of plants that you can grow at home. Organizations like the Cactus and Succulent Society of America (see page 113) are another great source for seeds. They offer seed exchanges that often include many interesting species as a benefit of membership. Another fun way to get started is to pick up a packet of seeds at a garden shop. The only drawback is that seed packets usually contain an assortment of different cacti or succulents, which can be frustrating if you would like to know the names of the plants you have grown.

Don't forget to investigate your own plants. Some succulents make seed collection very easy because their fruits dry and pop open on their own. After removing any chaff collected with the seeds, store them in a small seed envelope or film canister labeled with the plant name and date, and keep them in a cool, dark place until you're ready to sow. Some cacti produce seeds in a pulpy fruit. Often the ripe fruit splits open itself, or you can cut it in half yourself. Scoop out the pulp, rinse off the seeds,

and allow them to dry. If properly stored, most seeds remain viable for up to three years. You may want to keep a garden journal in which to record your successes or failures and the important dates in your seeds' journey to planthood.

STARTING SEED

It is best to sow your seeds in the beginning of the growing season, which for most succulents is the spring. When you're ready to sow seeds, start with a good-quality soil mix. A sterile seed-starting mix is the best

Cacti started from seed grow best when several plantlets occupy one pot, such as the _Stenocactus_ (_Echinofossulocactus_) _coptonogonus_ seedlings shown here.

option because it helps avoid fungus problems after the seeds germinate. Next, fill a clean plastic pot, seed tray, or flat with soil mix, and thoroughly drench it with water. How deep should you plant the seed? A general rule of thumb is to gauge the seed's diameter and plant it twice as deep. Sprinkle very fine seed on top of the soil.

Put the container in a shallow pan of water. It's a good way to keep the soil moist without overhead watering, which disturbs the seeds. Cover the pot with plastic or glass to retain the moisture in the soil, but open it periodically to allow some air in. Place the container in a bright location and keep the soil mixture warm, somewhere between 60ºF and 80ºF. Some people put their seed pots on heating mats or on top of their refrigerator to ensure that the soil stays warm. Once you see little seedlings, permanently remove the cover and give the plantlets some air. Place them in brighter light and keep the growing medium moist but not wet. Gradually start to water less and find the seedlings an even brighter location, if possible.

The next step calls for patience. Allow your seedlings to grow bigger without being disturbed. It seems that succulent seedlings like to be in close proximity to each other, so don't move them into separate containers until they are very crowded and even touching. When you do transplant them, to save space and avoid overwatering, move two or three little plants into one three-inch pot filled with a well-draining potting mix. Hold each plantlet by a leaf and use a plastic fork to gently ease the small root systems out of the pot. Try not to touch or disturb the root system any more than you have to. Use the handle of your fork to make a hole for the roots in the new pot and gently accommodate the plantlet in its new home. Then label the pot with the plant name and date. The entire process from sowing seed to transplanting seedlings could take anywhere from six months to a year—maybe even more. Again, a garden journal to document your plant's progress may be helpful.

Cuttings

For faster results, cuttings are the way to go. With very little effort, you can have a fully formed new plant in a month or two. In fact, for many succulents, asexual propagation is part of their natural survival strategy. Jumping cholla (*Opuntia fulgida*) has segmented stems that easily break (or "jump") off when an animal or person bumps into it. Once it lands on the ground, the segment will eventually root itself. This has proven to be a very effective means of survival, for jumping chollas are a ubiquitous element of the landscape in the Southwest.

STEM CUTTINGS

Succulents like echeverias, sedums, and kalanchoes have aerial roots along their stems and are ready-made for cuttings. Simply cut off a piece of stem below some roots. Ideally the stem should be between a half and one inch long, but it can be shorter if needed. Before planting, allow the cut end to callus over in a warm and dry location, which may take a week or two. This helps prevent fungal infections. When the cutting is ready, pot it in a very porous rooting medium. I start with a sterile houseplant potting mix that contains perlite and add more perlite at a ratio of two parts perlite to one part potting mix. Water whenever the medium becomes dry until the cutting has developed a sizeable root ball (there will be evidence of new growth above ground). Then repot the plant in a well-draining cactus soil mix. Take all cuttings in the spring, and keep them in warm bright light with good air circulation.

You can follow the above procedure even if the plant does not have any aerial roots. Make your cut below a leaf node (the scar where a leaf or stem once was), and after it calluses, plant the cutting with the leaf node beneath the soil surface. Of course, it will take a little longer for a root system to develop.

To propagate prickly pear cactus, gently remove one or more pads from a vigorous plant and let the cut end of each pad callus over before placing it in growing medium. Roots should form within several weeks.

If you remove a leaf from a succulent like *Kalanchoe beharensis* (left) or *Kalanchoe tomentosa* (right) and stick it into soil, a new plant should form at the base of the leaf in a few months.

LEAF CUTTINGS

Succulents like echeverias, gasterias, and opuntias can be propagated from a leaf (or, in the case of *Opuntia,* a pad) or even part of a leaf. Remove a leaf, allow it to callus, and plant it in rooting medium. With longer leaves like those of a *Sansevieria,* you can actually cut the leaf into sections and plant those. Soon little plantlets will form at the base of the larger leaf cutting. Gently remove each plantlet as you would a seedling, by gently grasping it by the leaf and lifting it from the soil by hand or with a plastic fork, disturbing the root system as little as possible. Eventually, the original plant piece will fall away, or you can remove it yourself.

REJUVENATING SUCCULENTS

Leaf and stem cuttings are also an effective way to rejuvenate succulents that have become too leggy or unsightly. Taking cuttings often encourages newer, fuller growth in the original plant and enables you to make a new plant from the cuttings.

Offsets

Clumping succulents, such as some aloes, agaves, sempervivums, gasterias, and some cacti, form offsets, which may have tiny roots at their bases. Carefully remove the offset intact and, after any necessary callusing, plant it in a rooting medium. If the offset has roots already, plant it directly in soil. To avoid overwatering, use the smallest pot that fits the plant and is heavy enough to provide a sturdy base.

Divisions

Dividing succulents like sedums or delospermas is done in much the same way as with garden perennials. With a small potted plant, you can cut the root ball in half with a clean knife and repot the sections. If the plant is in the ground, lift the plant and try to gently separate the root ball with a shovel. Always thoroughly water any newly potted or replanted division immediately.

Grafting

Grafting is a more challenging propagation technique, primarily done in nurseries to enable faster growth of slow-growing or difficult cacti. Grafting joins a desirable (but usually fussy) top portion, or scion, to a fast-growing rootstock such as night-blooming cereus, *Hylocereus undatus.* Grafting can be an effective way to make cacti that would rot out in wet-winter areas, such as *Sclerocactus* and *Pediocactus,* more moisture-resistant.

There are two basic methods of grafting: flat and cleft. To do a flat graft, cut off the top of the stock plant with a clean knife, and then make downward diagonal cuts (or bevels) along the edges of the stock plant. This will help make a tighter fit between the two plants. Then cut the scion in the same way. Gently press the two pieces together so that there are no gaps for air to enter and fasten the two together with a rubber band. Leave the grafted plant in a bright place for two weeks, then check to see if the graft has taken. If it hasn't, start over again by making new cuts.

To create a cleft graft, make a V-shaped incision in the rootstock plant and cut a wedge in the scion so that it fits into the V-shaped incision. Then tie the two together by wrapping some string (or a few rubber bands) around the top of the stock plant and the bottom of the pot in a couple of directions, much like a piece of ribbon around a gift box. This will keep the graft secure. Try to keep the plants dry when watering to reduce the risk of rot. It may be fun to experiment with grafting to develop a new skill, but the end result can be, alas, a very strange-looking plant.

Fewer than 200 plants of the Mexican native *Mammillaria luethyi* survive in the wild, where the species is endangered by illegal collection. The specimen shown here was grafted—a fast way to make more plants for the trade. Each of the new plant bodies is suitable as a scion.

Whatever methods you try, you will discover that propagating succulents offers much satisfaction and enrichment.

Succulent Bonsai: Creating Dramatic Miniature Trees

Susan Amoy

In ancient Chinese culture, great landscape features—mountains, hills, and bodies of water—were attributed with supernatural power. Their life force, or chi, was believed to permeate all things and vitalize living matter. To embody the essence of chi in an intimate setting and to express harmony with nature, *penjing*—the pursuit of re-creating nature in miniature—was developed and became the precurser of Japanese bonsai. Though traditional styles were created with deciduous and evergreen trees in mind, they can be applied to succulents to create unique and dramatic bonsai specimens. Succulents have many appealing features, such as interesting bark texture and color, fabulous foliage, and tuberous roots, as well as swollen bases, trunks, and branches. Some species like *Tylecodon cacalioides* are naturally small in scale; others like *Bursera fagaroides* are often dwarfed in nature by environmental conditions. Many are beautiful in seasonal flower or display dramatic form when dormant and leafless. Some types are pleasantly aromatic. The tremendous range in shape and form of the roughly 10,000 species of succulents allows bonsai artists to shape unique and memorable specimens resembling magnificent aged trees, often with fascinating engorged or twisted roots or trunks, suggestive of the harsh conditions in the plants' native environments.

Clockwise from top left: To highlight its attractive bark, *Pseudobombax ellipticum* can be grown to form a round base; *Pachypodium baronii* var. *windsorii* is staged in a rugged rock to suggest its native limestone habitat in Madagascar; for a great visual effect, the massive tuber of *Fockea edulis* is mostly exposed; *Tylecodon cacalioides* is grown with multiple trunks to give the specimen presence and mass.

Magnificent, aged trees like this baobab, *Adansonia digitata*, at Epupa Falls on the border between Angola and Namibia, inspire bonsai artists to train unique specimens in miniature.

Growing Succulent Bonsai

Understanding the conditions in the individual species' habitats and approximating them at home is essential to growing healthy, long-lived, and well-formed succulent bonsai specimens.

GROWING MEDIA, CONTAINERS, AND MULCHES Healthy roots make for healthy plants. The requirements for a growing medium for succulent plants are very similar to bonsai soil: noncompacting, generally neutral pH, and porous for good drainage and aeration. A good basic recipe appears on page 91. As with all bonsai, the container should complement the bonsai as a frame complements a painting. Succulents may be staged as individual bonsai, forests, companion plants, or in landscape trays. For obvious reasons, avoid planting species that have different growing requirements together in the same container. Do not use moss, because it doesn't typically grow with desert plants and therefore presents an unnatural setting (in addition to having very different moisture needs). Use crushed rock, fired clay, or gravel to cover the soil. In addition to securing the plants to the container with wire ties, you can use rocks to prop and stabilize the plants. Above all, ensure good drainage. Drill additional holes as needed, and cover all holes with nonclogging screen.

Soil Mix for Succulent Bonsai

The following recipe is a good basic mix for succulent bonsai. For a more moisture-retentive growing medium, increase the amount of organics and/or decrease particle size:

- 1 part aggregate such as crushed quartz, decomposed granite, or Haydite (high-fired clay)
- 1 part Turface, crushed cinder, or pumice
- 1 part organic material: bark chips, peat, or coir

Blend well and add per cubic foot of mix:

- A handful of crushed coral (make sure there is no salt residue), gypsum, or bone meal to provide calcium
- A small handful of medium laden with mycorrhizae to stimulate root function (optional but helpful)

LIGHT AND TEMPERATURES Succulent bonsai enjoy a warm, well-lit, non-humid growing environment with good air circulation. To remain healthy they need the equivalent of a half to a full day of slightly shaded or full sun. In general it's best to keep them at temperatures above 50°F. If seasonal temperatures drop lower, a heated greenhouse or well-lit indoor growing area is required.

WATERING When watering, drench the growing medium completely until water drips from the drainage holes in the container. Let the soil dry out completely or almost completely before watering again. Some species have a seasonal growth pattern, in which temperature change, photoperiod change, or drought triggers dormancy. Plants may drop their leaves as a signal. When a plant is dormant, reduce watering until new growth appears. Also note that plants use less water on cool, overcast days than on warm, clear days. Periodically spray leaves and stems to remove dust. Use a fertilizer with a 5-5-5 NPK ratio for slower growth or 14-14-14 for faster growth. To promote slow, even growth, it's best to apply small doses of fertilizer solution frequently. Dormant plants should not be fertilized.

Observe your plants carefully and look for signs of trouble: If a plant receives too little light, too much water, or too much fertilizer, it will respond with elongated trunks, stems, and internodes, and larger-than-normal leaves.

REPOTTING AND ROOT PRUNING Contrary to the practice for temperate and tropical bonsai species, succulent species should not be watered just after repotting. Watering bruised and reestablishing root systems of succulents invites rot. Wait several days or up to several weeks before watering, then keep watering to a minimum until new growth appears. For health reasons, root pruning is not recommended or needed in succulent species. Succulent roots are rarely vigorous after being pruned, and the less disruption they experience the better. If they are trimmed for aesthetic reasons, remove all soil and let the cuts and roots dry until completely callused before replanting; this may require several weeks for very large cuts. Moisture on an open succulent wound almost certainly invites rot.

Unusual and rare, this *Euphorbia* 'Hummel's Hybrid' is an aged, crested specimen displaying convoluted growth patterns.

Styling Succulent Bonsai

The art of styling bonsai lies in understanding the methodology of styling, then applying it to the individual plant in a way that emphasizes its best features so that artificially directed growth appears natural and interesting. Some succulent bonsai may resemble the more familiar bonsai conifers and temperate deciduous trees. Other forms defy traditional styles and, in some cases, challenge our definitions of what makes a tree. (For more information on the art and techniques of bonsai styling, consult a good general guidebook.)

COLUMNAR STYLE Some adult succulent trees have evolved a massive, moisture-filled trunk that extends upward from base to canopy like a column. The trunk may extend for two-thirds or more of the total height of the tree and is crowned by usually sparse branches and foliage, flowers, and fruit. Examples of this form can be found in adult *Pachypodium lamerei, P. geayi, Adansonia grandidieri, Moringa drouhardii,* and *M. hildebrantii.*

BOTTLE-SHAPE STYLE Many succulents also display a mature form with the trunk swollen at the base and midsection like a wine bottle, flask, or sometimes, a sphere. These trunks will form a reverse taper—that is, the base of the trunk or root area will be narrower in girth than the section above it, which swells out before tapering again toward the top where the branches appear. Though this is not an acceptable aesthetic in traditional Oriental bonsai, it is quite common—and natural—in succulent forms. Examples of this form can be found in some species of adult *Brachychiton, Bursera,* and *Adansonia* trees and *Beaucarnea stricta, Pachypodium gracilus,* and *Adenium obesum.*

Wiring Succulent Bonsai

Wiring gives the bonsai artist more options to manipulate growth. Using this technique, an existing trunk or branch can be wrapped with spirals of wire, then bent into the desired shape. The wires will hold the plant in the new form. Over time, the wires can be removed, and the plant will maintain its new form without their support.

Aluminum wire is recommended for succulents. It is more pliable than copper wire, which may bruise succulents. You may need to leave wires on for long periods of time, because succulents are generally slow growing. Wiring can stay on as long as it is not cutting into the branch and until the branch has set and holds it shape. You can use guy wires to tie a trunk or branch to the container, to a stake, or

Aluminum wires covered with aquarium air-line tubing gently mold an *Operculicarya decaryi* into the desired shape.

to some other part of the plant to change its shape and hold it in place. Similarly, you can tie weights to a branch to pull it down to a new angle. To prevent bruising, slip aquarium air-line tubing over the wire. Do not use raffia, plastic, or other coverings that may hold water and encourage rot.

As with traditional bonsai, it is best to wind the wire in 45-degree-angle bends for optimum holding strength. Try to leave air space about the thickness of a playing card or credit card between bark and wire. In this way, the tree can grow and expand a little, and the wire will not mark the bark. If you wrap the wire too tightly, it will very quickly scar the bark. Avoid crossing wires: They don't hold well, look ugly, are more difficult to remove, and may leave crisscross scars. Keep a close eye on the wired area, and remove any wiring before it cuts into the bark. Remember, you can always rewire it if a branch has not yet settled into its new position.

Easy Bonsai for Beginners

Succulent species that lend themselves to bonsai and are relatively simple to care for are those that tolerate a greater range of growing conditions, such as varying levels of light and watering. They branch readily when pruned, grow relatively quickly, and are fairly easy to propagate and therefore widely available commercially.

Relatively fast growing, easy to maintain, and suitable for most bonsai styles, *Adenium obesum* grows into a rewarding miniature tree within a few years.

What to Look for When Buying Plants

In general, pick a healthy and established succulent that's slow growing or has a dwarf habit and a potentially long life span. The plant should be well rooted, acclimatized to your growing environment, and suited to life in the confinement of a container. It should transplant well, since maintenance will require periodic repotting. Choose plants in which growth can be directed and a desired shape can be maintained. The plant should have a desirable growth habit, displaying a treelike adult form. If you are training an upright tree, choose a species that grows upright. If you are training a horizontal or cascading style, pick a plant with a similar growth habit or a species that will maintain a horizontal shape. The succulent's branches should be well placed, or it should be possible to direct them into a pleasing shape as the plant matures. (Be sure to choose a species that sprouts new growth after it has been pruned so that new growth can be directed.) In addition, look for internodes, leaves, flowers, and fruit that are small enough to appear in scale to a plant in miniature. Finally, look for dramatic or interesting visual features: form, texture, pattern, flower, fruit, foliage, bark, branch formation, or root formation.

Adenium obesum Desert Rose, Impala Lily

Suitable for most bonsai styles, *Adenium obesum* is a relatively fast grower: a seedling can develop into a rewarding bonsai in as little as five years. Many specimens develop interesting large, twisted bases and roots, which are partially exposed and displayed. Profuse two- to three-inch variations of fuchsia-pink flowers with white throats cover the plant when it is in active growth. Branches can be wired and growing tips pruned or pinched to encourage branching and compact growth. A common offering from cactus and succulent specialty nurseries, and sometimes available at garden shops, this species thrives in full, all-day sun but will tolerate lower light conditions; it can be grown as an indoor bonsai if excellent indoor light is provided. It doesn't require a dormant period but will go into dormancy if kept cooler or exposed to a shorter day length or drought. To maintain growth, keep it at 75°F to 100°F and water moderately and evenly, letting the soil dry almost completely between waterings. Fertilize lightly regularly while the plant is growing. Propagate from seed, grafts, and (with some difficulty) from branch cuttings. There are several other species of *Adenium* available and many hybrids.

Bursera fagaroides Elephant Tree

Bursera fagaroides is a Sonoran Desert species related to myrrh. The aromatic resins of *Bursera* have been used medicinally, to make copal, and to bind paint pigments.

Seedlings and specimens are available from cactus and succulent nurseries. The branches, trunk, and base hold reserves of water for the plant, thus becoming engorged with age. In the wild, specimens are often twisted and gnarled by the wind and desert conditions where they grow. Branches are very flexible and easy to wire. This species responds well to pruning with increased branching. Leaves are small, and fruit and flowers are inconspicuous. It is relatively slow growing: A specimen with a trunk diameter of four inches may be over 30 years old. Grow at 70ºF to 100ºF in full all-day sun, with moderate water. Dormancy is not required but will be signaled by dropping of all leaves with the onset of cooler

Bursera fagaroides before becoming a bonsai specimen, top, and after three years of training, bottom: Branches are tapered and wired to achieve a more attractive placement, and the plant has been installed at a slightly more dramatic angle.

temperatures, shorter day length, or drought. If kept small, these trees can be grown as indoor bonsai under excellent indoor lighting. Propagate from seed and (with some difficulty) from branch and larger root cuttings. Although used for upright growing styles, *Bursera fagaroides* makes excellent prostrate and windblown specimens.

Crassula ovata Jade Plant

A common houseplant, xeric landscape plant, and staple at cactus and succulent nurseries, *Crassula ovata* makes a good medium to large-size bonsai. It can be wired, but because branches and trunk are more succulent than woody, it lends itself well to the "clip-and-grow" technique. Leaves and branches are brittle and break easily if handled roughly. The plant thrives on full all-day sun but can be raised with good indoor lighting. It is relatively fast growing; however if given too much water and fertilizer and not enough light, the plant will etiolate and the leaves will become artificially large. If grown well, the tree will bloom with pink flowers. It can be propagated easily from callused cuttings placed in moderately moist soil. Use it for upright bonsai styles and multiple tree plantings.

Operculicarya decaryi

Native to Madagascar, this increasingly popular species (pictured on page 93) is now propagated in domestic cactus and succulent nurseries and makes excellent bonsai material. It is suitable for upright, informal upright, slanted, and windblown bonsai styles. Its small compound leaves, good branch development, and warty bark are attractive bonsai characteristics. The young trunks and most branches are highly flexible and can be wired and positioned easily. Grow in half- to three-quarter-day full or partially muted sunlight, or under good indoor lights. As long as it is growing and healthy, this species enjoys slightly more moist conditions than many other succulents and doesn't like to have its soil completely dry out. Growing fairly fast, this plant can make a small bonsai in a few years. It can be propagated with some difficulty from branch and root cuttings. Keep it at 65°F to 110°F.

Portulacaria afra Miniature Jade Plant

This small-leafed plant is an excellent candidate for upright styles and multiple tree plantings. The bark is reddish on young growth and turns crusty red or gray as it ages.

Branches and young trunks can be wired or trained in the "clip-and-grow" method, and when pruned regularly, they rebranch well. A fast grower, the species thrives in full sun, with even, moderately moist soil conditions. It can tolerate partially muted sunlight and excellent indoor lights. Keep at temperatures of 50° F to 100° F. It is propagated easily from callused cuttings placed in moist soil.

This *Crassula ovata* 'Gollum', a cultivated monstrose form of the jade plant, has been trained to develop three trunks.

What makes a prizewinner? Clockwise from top left, the *Melocactus matanzanus*, crested *Echinopsis*, and *Euphorbia squarrosa* are not only beautiful plants but are also presented to best effect. The *Stenocactus multicostatus*, at bottom left, is lovely, but the unflattering pot and lack of topdressing would lose it points in a competition.

Grooming Cacti and Other Succulents for Exhibition

Ray Rogers

I admit it: I'm hooked on exhibiting plants. Show me a coleus or a cactus, and I start thinking about its possibilities as a show plant. However, I can imagine the questions arising in many readers' minds: Why should I bother to grow a show plant, especially when there's no show nearby to compete in? What is a show plant, anyway? What's in it for me?

Of course, competing in a show can win you a ribbon or two, or, if you keep at it for more than a few years, hundreds of them. But there's more to competition than amassing ribbons and trophies; most veteran exhibitors will tell you that it's the camaraderie among fellow exhibitors that keeps them coming back for more. Also, a well-run show is a tremendous educational experience for both the participants and the visitors, some of whom may be inspired to join in the fun. Arguably the most compelling reason for raising show plants is having well-grown plants around to enjoy, regardless of whether they make it to a show (much less win awards).

So how exactly is a show plant different from an ordinary plant? You might think the difference lies in a show plant's age or rarity, or maybe it must be covered with flowers or fruit, or perhaps it's been trained into a fantastic shape or has required years of careful cultivation to bring it to near perfection. These and other traits certainly do elevate show plants to special status, but often the difference between a top award and a lesser one (or none at all) comes down to two major factors: good cultivation (which is not addressed here) and attention to details.

Preparing a Plant for Show

You may have a well-tended cactus or other succulent in your collection, but unless it's been groomed ("dressed up") for competition and presented looking its best, chances are good it's not going to fare well in a show. Grooming a plant for a show begins with a plant inspection and cleanup.

In general, anything that spoils the overall good looks of a plant needs to vanish. But be sure to stay within reason when you set to work: Don't strip off too much, or you will ruin the appearance of the plant and perhaps even kill it. Discard any off-color and damaged plant parts such as yellowing leaves or broken stems and spines. Remove any dying or dead foliage as well as fading, wilting, and similarly less than optimal flowers and fruit. Also take off any leaves, flowers, or fruit that are dramatically larger or smaller than the rest.

Sometimes plants, especially cacti, are affected by a condition referred to as "creeping crud." It starts as an off-color area near the base. The affected area eventually appears scarred or becomes sunken, greatly detracting from the plant's show-worthiness. Creeping crud can sometimes be hidden by setting a plant a little lower in its pot or covering any unsightly areas with topdressing (see below).

Check your plant, especially if it's a single-bodied cactus, for constricted or elongated areas. Impossible to hide, they often indicate that the plant received inadequate light or fertilizer at some point in its life. Proper care usually restores good growth but will not correct flaws in form. Start with another plant and be consistent in your care.

Stay on the lookout for pests and diseases, and treat them if they occur. Most shows will reject a potential entry if a problem is detected.

Grooming Basics

With experience, every exhibitor discovers the tools and methods that best suit his or her own needs, but it's safe to say that most exhibitors start with a pair of small, sharp scissors to remove small stuff and to trim leaves; pruners for more substantial cuts; a pair or two of tweezers to pull out dead leaves; and nimble fingers. Your own hands can be the best, most versatile tools you have at your disposal, but be careful: Tugging at a plant part instead of cutting it may tear off more than just the offending bit or leave an ugly scar.

Adopt a triage approach to cleaning up a long-neglected plant. First remove the most unsightly and noticeable debris, then go back over the entire plant and take

To look its best for competition, *Aloe* 'Lizard Lips' gets a cleanup: Spent flowers, tattered foliage, and debris are removed, and the plant is presented in a more attractive pot.

out the smaller, less visible material. Take a break from your plant for a while, and then return to it with fresh eyes for a final, very refined session before you enter it in a show.

Of Pots and Plants

How a plant is presented in its pot makes a big contribution to the overall quality of the exhibit. Start by matching the size of the container to the size of the plant. Then position the plant in the center of the pot at the proper depth: An off-center plant looks sloppy, and a plant that sits too low in its pot, especially if it's a single-bodied cactus or mound of clumping succulents, looks as if it is trying to hide. On the other hand, a plant that sits too high in its pot looks like it's trying to jump out. Don't be afraid to repot a plant into a new container—even at practically the last minute—if doing so makes the overall entry look better. Be careful when repotting, though: Some cacti and other succulents are rather fragile.

It's not just the container that comes into play when presenting a plant in its best light. If a plant does not completely cover the growing medium in a pot—and particularly when the medium is speckled with perlite or tiny weeds—then steps must be taken to disguise the imperfections of the medium and present a more pleasing, uniform surface. Topdressing an entry is perhaps the easiest of all the operations in preparing a show plant, but it is often the weak spot. My best advice is to keep it simple and use a material that's subtle, relatively uniform in texture and color, and heavy enough to stay in place if watered or gently jostled. Brown or black aquarium gravel or rather coarse sand meets all of these requirements (see also page 69).

Some shows declare themselves to be "pot neutral." The judges in these shows are not supposed to consider the color, shape, surface, or other attributes of an entry's container when making their decisions. Even if the judges are observing neutrality, you can bet your last blue ribbon that an entry presenting a plant in a clean pot in a complementary color and shape will beat an entry that has a plant in a dirty or unflattering pot, even if the two plants themselves are identical in appearance.

Show plants are, for the most part, the pampered recipients of continuous brushing, cleaning, and trimming, much like the entries at a dog show or county-fair cattle show. Unlike dogs or cattle, however, plants don't move unless someone picks them up. The successful exhibitor takes advantage of this by choosing a show plant's best side and then making the effort to present it to advantage. The difference between a winner and a third-place ribbon usually lies in the exhibitor's ability to minimize imperfections, whether by carefully removing them, lessening their size, hiding them with another plant

Every detail counts: The glaucous coating on a few lower leaves of this *Echeveria laui* has been marred by touching, making the plant unsuitable for competition unless the damaged leaves can be removed or hidden.

part, or by positioning the plant so that its faults are not easily detected by the judges.

Transport your entries carefully in boxes or crates or by surrounding the pots with paper or old clothes or similar padding—jostling and sudden stops can topple top-heavy plants. And to make sure spiny cacti don't stab the plants next to them, pack them in individual carriers.

CAN YOU DO IT?

By now, you may be thinking that a great deal of time, effort, and showmanship is required to turn out a spectacular ribbon-winning plant. While it's true that many prizewinners have been in their owners' care for many years, it is possible to buy a well-grown plant

The author's good care and grooming were rewarded with several ribbons for his *Dioscorea mexicana*.

a few months before a show (but make sure you honor the requirements for length of ownership) and then spend a little time dressing it up. Virtually everyone who exhibits cacti and other succulents can relate stories of undemanding plants that required very little special effort to grow and groom into beautiful specimens. Successful showmanship comes with experience, but even beginners can succeed if they follow the basics of good care and presentation.

See you at the show!

Green Roofs: New Homes for Sedums and Other Hardy Succulents

Edmund C. Snodgrass

There is a new landscape emerging in North America, still largely unseen but gaining in popularity. That landscape is the green roof. Green roofs have started sprouting in urban areas everywhere, giving some of our favorite hardy succulents new opportunities to shine. Sedums and ice plants are the stars of many green roofs: Tolerant of heat, sun, wind, drought, salt, disease, and insects, these low-growing, shallow-rooted workhorses of the perennial plant world have what it takes to thrive in the tough conditions high atop multistory buildings.

One form of roof garden has been a popular design element for public spaces like parking garages and museums in North America for the last 50 years. In the lexicon of green roofs it's known as the intensive green roof. These roofs are constructed with a layer of growing medium most often measured in feet, not inches, and have elaborate irrigation systems as well as substantial maintenance budgets. Intensive green roofs have the look and feel of traditional gardens despite their higher elevation.

More recently, a second type of roof garden has come into existence, one that has the potential to benefit the environment in addition to soothing the eye. The extensive green roof is typically created with three to six inches of growing medium, has no irri-

Perfectly suited to the harsh growing conditions on top of buildings, hardy succulents like sedums and ice plants are elements of many environmentally sound roof designs.

gation system, has a very limited or no maintenance budget, and generally serves a practical, rather than mostly aesthetic, purpose. All year long, the extensive green roof soaks up stormwater that would otherwise run off, taxing city sewer systems and damaging receiving waterways. Extensive green roofs also help lower ambient temperatures during the summer months, lowering cooling costs and helping to mitigate the so-called urban heat island effect.

Many European countries, most notably Germany and Switzerland, have embraced extensive green roof designs for practical, environmental, and aesthetic purposes. As the boundaries of growing cities rush to merge with the countryside, constructing green roofs has become an important way to reduce the impact of ever-increasing impervious surfaces. By virtue of their planted areas, extensive roofs green and cool cities, increase oxygen output, soften urban streetscapes, and reduce stormwater runoff to vital tributaries and major bodies of water that supply drinking water to millions of people across Europe. So serious are northern European concerns about the environmental impacts of development that federal laws mandate that development must be offset by green spaces; as a result, 14 percent of Germany's flat roofs now sport green roofs.

North America lags far behind Europe in this regard. Urban jurisdictions are still coming to grips with major stormwater-management issues that are directly linked to the rapid spread of roads, pavement, and other impervious surfaces over the last 30 years. This, in turn, has left aging water and sewer systems prone to regular flooding, which has a serious impact on the quality of water in our rivers and streams. Because of this, there is tremendous pressure from both government regulators and citizen environmental advocates to address issues of stormwater management in a meaningful way. But how do you help cities that have been designed to shed water as rapidly as possible become capable of absorbing rainwater? Green roofs are the obvious answer. Studies conducted on green roofs over a three-year period by Bill Hunt and others at North Carolina State University, in Raleigh, have shown annual rainfall retention on an extensive green roof with a four-inch-deep growing medium to be around 60 percent. In addition to reducing the amount of stormwater runoff and lowering the summertime air temperature around buildings, green roofs also clean particulate matter out of the air, mitigate acid rain, extend the life of roof membranes by protecting them from harmful rays that are the primary cause of degradation, and perform many other site-specific functions, depending on design and region.

In England, for example, urban green roofs are being used to provide habitat for insects and nesting areas for birds like the black redstart, which have lost substantial habitat to development. Other buildings feature green roofs to boost worker productivity in offices—studies have shown that worker absenteeism is lower in buildings that are environmentally friendly, for example. Best of all, these benefits occur simultaneously, and collectively they give building owners a return on their investment of installing the extra layers that make up the green roof. As the measurable benefits are being quantified, public officials in the U.S. and Canada are beginning to embrace green roofs as an important tool in improving the quality of life in urban areas. One by one, local jurisdictions are giving incentives such as tax breaks to encourage green roofs and reduce the adverse effects of development. Look for many more green roofs to come.

Green Roof Basics

Deciding whether to plant a green roof should begin with a series of questions designed to pinpoint its primary function. Is the green roof purely aesthetic in nature, offering a green respite in a sea of asphalt? Is it intended to deal with stormwater runoff, in which case aesthetics might be a secondary consideration to water retention? Is the roof designed to have a therapeutic effect, say, as an installation atop a hospital, where patients might visit? Is it largely educational in nature, open to the public and serving to teach people about the benefits that green roofs offer?

Planted with hardy succulents, a green roof serves many useful purposes: It helps cool the building in summer, absorbs a substantial portion of rainwater, and extends the lifetime of the roof membrane.

Funky as well as functional, a green roof easily integrates the shed with its foliage-clad neighbors and significantly extends the space for low-maintenance gardening.

Determining the purpose of the green roof will help to determine a number of things, among them the most suitable plants, whether or not you'll need an irrigation system, and how much load the roof must bear and whether it needs to be retrofitted to accommodate the extra weight of the medium and the plants.

An extensive green roof with a planting medium between two and six inches in depth adds between 14 and 35 pounds per square foot. This is a substantial increase of weight, and a structural engineer should be consulted to make sure that an existing roof can accommodate the extra weight, or if not, how it can be retrofitted to do so. In the case of new construction, load bearing should be factored in at the design phase and worked out between architect and engineer. An engineer can also calculate other additional loads associated with a green roof, including live load, which factors in human foot traffic, temporary installations of furniture, and so on. Your architect or contractor should be aware of any special requirements in your area, including whether a building permit is needed to construct a green roof and whether there are any tax or other incentives for doing so.

Once you've determined the purpose of your roof and structural issues, you will need to find a reputable and experienced company that has worked on green roofs previously and is familiar with the necessary layers that each green roof requires. Briefly, those components include decking, waterproofing, insulation, drainage, filter cloth, medium, and, finally, plants. There are complete green roof systems available (mostly from German companies that have entered the North American market), or the green roof can be built layer by layer by a roofing contractor. Plan your roof for a minimum 30-year life span—it's costly and impractical to need to rip up the garden because of a failing in the roofing materials. (For more information on the structural elements of installing a green roof, see *Planting Green Roofs and Living Walls*, Nigel Dunett and Nöel Kingsbury, Timber Press, 2004.)

When it's finally time to start thinking about plants, you need to decide how much time and money to allocate for maintenance. Grasses, for example, must be cut back periodically to avoid becoming a fire hazard. Some plants need regular pruning, watering, or fertilization. You will also need to know how and when you will access the roof. If access is limited or there is no one to perform the maintenance needed for some plants, then you'll want to choose plants with minimal requirements.

Rooftop Environments

Rooftop growing conditions are usually much harsher than those found on the ground in the same area. For example, winds are much fiercer 20 stories above ground than they are at street level; they can quickly desiccate the plants and growing medium. To pick the right plants for the job, get to know the microclimate of your rooftop environment. As a first step, determine the minimum and maximum roof temperatures and observe how sunlight travels across the roof, noting if any sections are shaded by trees or other buildings for part or all of the day. Knowing the relative amounts of sun and shade the roof receives will help you pick plants that are most compatible with particular areas.

In general, green-roof plants should be ecologically compatible, fast growing but not invasive, and fire resistant. To avoid interfering with the well-being of the roof, they should also be long-lived or self-propagating, have shallow, fibrous root systems, and be lightweight when fully grown. As a rule, hardy succulent groundcovers are excellent candidates for green roofs, and of those, *Sedum* is the most versatile and common genus used. Sedums thrive in dry conditions and nutrient-poor soils, require little to no maintenance, and resist being blown over by wind because of their short stature. Many low-growing species and cultivars are available, and together with evergreen plants they can be arranged into interesting patterns that provide aesthetically pleasing roofscapes year-round.

Although it is not generally the case, in some circumstances, it may be desirable or necessary to irrigate an extensive green roof. It's doubtful, for example, that a green roof could survive in the arid Southwest without some kind of installed irrigation system for the hottest and driest months. Similarly, if you wanted to mix more demanding plants such as herbaceous perennials with the dominant succulents and grasses, it might be necessary to irrigate the roof (and increase the depth of the medium) to allow the less drought-tolerant species to flourish. Irrigating a green roof greatly expands the plant choices available to you, but it also increases the weight of the roof, the cost, and the need for maintenance. A variety of systems is available and should be thoroughly researched or discussed with a knowledgeable expert.

To help choose plants that meet your site's needs, it's best to consult a professional horticulturist, landscape architect, or local nursery business familiar with selecting plants for green roofs in your area. The vast majority of plants found on extensive green roofs are hardy succulents, including *Delosperma, Jovibarba, Sempervivum,* and, as noted above, *Sedum.* With more than 600 species of *Sedum* alone, the choices are extensive and varied and can offer a prolonged period of bloom.

Rooftop Aesthetics

Green roofs can easily provide visual interest throughout the year, even in areas with very cold winters. The roofs are not evergreen in the strict sense of the word, but they do offer interest year-round. For example, *Sedum album* 'Murale' illustrates the versatility of the genus in a successful roof design. As this plant breaks dormancy in spring, it turns into a lush green carpet, increasing in vigor and growing out horizontally over time. Come early summer, terminal flower buds appear, obscuring the foliage under a haze of white flowers for about two weeks. Later on, the spent flower stalks continue to contribute visual interest, or they can be removed if desired. When fall approaches, the foliage slowly turns red, progressively darkening until it reaches a burgundy shade. It stays that way until it breaks dormancy the following spring.

Living roofs provide many options for playing with multiple permutations of colors and patterns. The key to creating a successful roof design is remembering that it needs to please from afar. Large broad-brush splashes of color stand out well at considerable distance, while small, intricate plant details get lost completely. The bright

Flowering from May all the way to October, *Phemeranthus calycinus* is an attractive North American native suitable for rooftop plantings.

red foliage of *Sedum spurium* 'Fuldaglut', for example, is a knockout from a distance, while the intricate details of the highly unusual gray foliage of *Orostachys boehmeri* can be appreciated only up close. (For low-growing sedums and other plants that offer superb foliage and flower colors, see "Great Succulents for Green Roofs," page 112.) Once you've selected low-growing sedums, you can add height, different textures, and colors to round out the design. Taller sedums like *Sedum sieboldii* or *S.* 'Matrona' work well, as do certain accent plants like *Dianthus* and *Phemeranthus* (syn. *Talinum*), which offer bright bursts of color when interspersed among other plants. Various ornamental onions (*Allium*) and short grasses like grama grass (*Bouteloua*) and sedges (*Carex*) can also be wonderful counterpoints to the hardy succulents that dominate the roof. Often, accent plants are not reliable enough to be dominant species, but if used wisely, they can add valuable interest to your green roof.

Depending on weather conditions, seasonal changes, and differences in climate from year to year, some plants will flourish, while others will recede. Some plants like *Allium* and *Phemeranthus* will self-seed from one year to the next, changing the garden's design. Over time, the unique landscape of your green roof will continue to evolve and change, even as it performs valuable services to your surroundings. With careful planning and a clever combination of groundcovers and accents, green roofs truly can provide a bright spot virtually year-round.

Great Succulents for Green Roofs

Combining fabulous foliage colors in broad sweeping patterns lies at the heart of an aesthetically successful green roof design, which will be viewed mostly from a considerable distance. Low-growing sedums and other closely related succulents offer a great palette to choose from: Their foliage comes in grays, blues, greens, reds, and yellows, as well as variegated forms, with many species and cultivars adding splashes of seasonal flowers and changing foliage hues as the seasons progress.

Sedums for Year-Round Interest

While not truly evergreen, these plants do not disappear in winter; rather, they assume winter colors from dark russet to brighter shades of red. During the growing season they form dense mats of green that are obscured only when they come into flower.

Sedum album and cultivars

Sedum hybridum 'Immergrünchen'

Sedum kamtschaticum 'Weihenstephaner Gold'

Sedum lanceolatum

Sedum sexangulare

Sedum sichotense

Sedum spurium 'Fuldaglut'

Sedum stefco

Sedum stenopetalum

Sedums With Blue Foliage

Sedum cauticola 'Lidakense'

Sedum hispanicum

Sedum ochroleucum

Sedum rupestre

Ever-Blooming Succulents

Some perennials act like annuals when it comes to blooming: Once they start—typically in late spring or early summer in most areas—they bloom continuously until frost or, in subtropical areas, year-round. South African ice plants (*Delosperma*) and North American *Phemeranthus* (syn. *Talinum*) species, native to serpentine prairie ecosystems, make first-rate perpetual bloomers.

Delosperma aberdeenense 'Abbey White'—white flowers

Delosperma brunnthaleri—yellow flowers

Delosperma cooperi—purple flowers

Delosperma floribundum 'Starburst'—purple flowers with white centers

Delosperma herbeum—white flowers

Delosperma ecklonis var. *latifolia*—purple flowers

Phemeranthus calycinus—purple flowers

Phemeranthus rugospermus—pink flowers

Nursery and Seed Sources

Abby Garden
P.O. Box 2249
La Habra, CA 90632-2249
562-905-3520

Bob Smoley's Gardenworld
3720 S.W. 183rd Terrace
Dunnellon, FL 34432
352-465-8254
www.bobsmoleys.com

Cactus and Succulent Plant Mall
www.cactus-mall.com

Cactus Limon
www.cactuslimon.com

Grigsby Cactus Gardens
2326-2354 Bella Vista Drive
Vista, CA 92084-7836
760-727-1323
www.cactus-mall.com/grigsby/

High Country Gardens
2902 Rufina Street
Santa Fe, NM
800-925-9387
www.highcountrygardens.com

Highland Succulents
1446 Bear Run Road
Gallipolis, OH 45631
740-256-1428
www.highlandsucculents.com

Intermountain Cactus
1478 North 750 East
Kaysville, UT 84037
801-546-2006

Lauray of Salisbury
432 Undermountain Road
Salisbury, CT 06068
860-435-2263
www.lauray.com

Living Stones Nursery
2936 North Stone Avenue
Tucson, AZ 85705

520-628-8773
www.lithops.net

Mesa Garden
P.O. Box 72
Belen, NM 87002
505-864-3131
www.mesagarden.com

Miles' to Go
P.O. Box 6
Cortaro, AZ 85652
520-682-7272
www.miles2go.com

Sacred Succulents
P.O. Box 781
Sebastopol, CA 95473
www.sacredsucculents.com

Shoal Creek Succulents
www.shoalcreeksucculents.com

Succulent Success Exotic Cacti Seeds
Asgardian Systems, Box 1142
Lake Cowichan, BC, V0R 2G0
Canada
250-749-7759
www.succulent success.com

The Cactus and Succulent Society of America

This international organization is dedicated to the knowledge, protection, and preservation of cacti and other succulents. Membership includes a subscription to *Cactus and Succulent Journal* and the newsletter *To the Point*, as well as the opportunity to obtain rare seeds at nominal cost from responsible sources and attend meetings, conferences, and shows with other cactophiles. Learn more about CSSA at http://www.cssainc.org.

Contributors

Susan Amoy developed her love of plants growing up in lush Hawaii. She now lives and works in the New York metropolitan area, where she specializes in bonsai with succulent plants and also maintains a selection of tropical and temperate bonsai. Susan is a member of the Cactus and Succulent Society of America and the Friends of Bonsai club at Brooklyn Botanic Garden, as well as other succulent and bonsai associations. For photographs of the artist's bonsai, visit www.susanamoy.com.

Susan Aument is curator of the Desert Collection, Tropical Entry House, and Trail of Evolution in the Steinhardt Conservatory at Brooklyn Botanic Garden. She has written about growing succulents indoors for BBG's *Plants & Gardens News.*

Gerald Barad, a retired gynecological surgeon, has been a collector and student of cacti and succulents for more than 50 years. He is an authority on the pollination and hybridization of the stapeliads. He was a founder and first president of the New York Cactus and Succulent Society and a past president and fellow of the Cactus and Succulent Society of America. Gerald traces his entry into the gardening world to his childhood days as a student in the children's program of BBG, when Ellen Eddy Shaw ran the program and Frances Miner was his teacher.

Panayoti Kelaidis is a plant explorer, gardener, and public garden administrator at Denver Botanic Gardens, where he is now director of outreach. He began his career at the garden in 1980 as curator of the rock alpine garden, where he designed and oversaw the initial plantings of the now extensive garden. He has a special passion for hardy cacti and is responsible for introducing most of the USDA Zone 5 hardy South African succulents currently in cultivation.

Stephen Maciejewski, a protective services social worker for the city of Philadelphia, spends his free time gardening outdoors or tending the countless plants growing on the windowsills and light carts throughout his home. Over the years he developed and perfected his growing and exhibiting skills and techniques by joining and participating in numerous local plant clubs, where he has held various leadership positions. Today, he's a fixture in the competitive division at the Philadelphia Flower Show Horticultural Court.

Janet Marinelli is director of Publishing at Brooklyn Botanic Garden. She has written extensively about conservation issues and believes that humble gardeners can be the true environmental heroes of the 21st century. Her latest book, *Plant* (Dorling Kindersley, 2005), showcases 2,000 species worldwide that are threatened in the wild but alive and well in gardens.

Sage Reynolds, an artist and designer, runs the Four Hands Design Studio, which he founded in 1977 with his partner, Colman Rutkin, in New York. He has been growing ceropegias and other succulent plants for more than 30 years. As a hobbyist, he has also hybridized azaleas, lilies, lithops, and abutilons.

Ray Rogers, a lifelong gardener, began his career in public horticulture, which led to a position as senior editor at Dorling Kindersley Publishing. Currently a freelance editor and author as well as an independent contractor for a local specialty nursery, Ray pursues his horticultural interests as a home gardener, as an amateur hybridizer of *Hippeastrum* (amaryllis), and as an award-winning exhibitor in the Philadelphia Flower Show. He is coauthor of *The Philadelphia Flower Show: Celebrating 175 Years* (HarperCollins, 2003).

Edmund C. Snodgrass is a horticulturist and fifth-generation farmer on Emory Knoll Farms, a 135-acre farm in Street, Maryland. He is the founding partner of Green Roof Plants, the only commercial nursery in the U.S. specializing in growing plants for green roofs, and has consulted on projects around the country and internationally. Currently, the nursery grows more than 300 plant varieties, including over 150 varieties of sedum.

Photos

Rob Cardillo all photos, except those noted below.

Charles Mann pages 8, 15, 18, 19, 21, 25, 26, 29, 31, 33

Sage Reynolds pages 12, 44, 47, 48, 51

Gerald Barad pages 13, 52, 53, 54, 55, 57, 58, 61

Christine Douglas page 16

Panayoti Kelaidis pages 17, 19

John Spain pages 22, 23

Stephen Maciejewski page 38, 103

Steve Casebolt page 66

Susan Amoy page 89 all, 92, 93, 96 both, 97

Dan Mahr page 90

Helena Fierlinger page 94

Edmund C. Snodgrass pages 104, 107, 108, 111

Index

More Books About Intriguing Plants

The Best Orchids for Indoors is a valuable introduction to these exquisite flowers and how they grow. Its beautifully photographed encyclopedia includes culture information and tips from experts about tropical orchids ideal for growing in the home.

Whether you are cultivating a few plants on a windowsill or nurturing an ever-expanding collection in the greenhouse, *The Gardener's Guide to Growing Orchids* is a perfect companion to *The Best Orchids for Indoors*. It includes step-by-step instructions on potting and repotting, watering, fertilizing, propagation, and more.

Ordering Books From Brooklyn Botanic Garden

World renowned for pioneering gardening information, Brooklyn Botanic Garden's award-winning guides provide practical advice for gardeners in every region of North America.

Join Brooklyn Botanic Garden as an annual Subscriber Member and receive three gardening handbooks, delivered directly to you, each year. Other benefits include free admission to many public gardens across the country, plus three issues of *Plants & Gardens News, Members News,* and our guide to courses and public programs.

For additional information about Brooklyn Botanic Garden, including other membership packages, call 718-623-7210 or visit our website at www.bbg.org. To order other fine titles published by BBG, call 718-623-7286 or shop in our online store at www.bbg.org/gardengiftshop.